SAM RAYBURN

Sam Rayburn circa 1948. Courtesy of the Sam Rayburn Library.

SAM RAYBURN

A Bio-Bibliography

Anthony Champagne

Bio-Bibliographies in Law and Political Science, Number 4

Greenwood Press
New York • Westport, Connecticut • London

Library of Congress Cataloging-in-Publication Data

Champagne, Anthony.
    Sam Rayburn : a bio-bibliography / Anthony Champagne.
       p.   cm. — (Bio-bibliographies in law and political science,
    ISSN 0882-7052 ; no. 4)
    Includes index.
    ISBN 0-313-25864-3 (lib. bdg. : alk. paper)
    1. Rayburn, Sam, 1882-1961. 2. Legislators—United States—
Biography. 3. United States. Congress. House—Biography.
4. Rayburn, Sam, 1882-1961—Bibliography. I. Title. II. Series.
E748.R24C48   1988
328.73′092′4—dc19   88-21341
    [B]

British Library Cataloguing in Publication Data is available.

Library of Congress Catalog Card Number: 88-21341
ISBN: 0-313-25864-3
ISSN: 0882-7052

First published in 1988

Greenwood Press, Inc.
88 Post Road West, Westport, Connecticut 06881

Printed in the United States of America

The paper used in this book complies with the
Permanent Paper Standard issued by the National
Information Standards Organization (Z39.48-1984).

10 9 8 7 6 5 4 3 2 1

Dedicated to

Michael and Peter

Contents

Preface

This book is intended for scholars interested in the life and times of Sam Rayburn. The biographical sketch provides an overview of Rayburn's life and work, and is followed by an annotated bibliography that describes many of the useful source materials on Rayburn. Only a brief section is devoted to Rayburn's writings because he did much of his work either on the telephone or in person. He did not write memoranda of conversations or agreements. The result is that many of his thoughts and decisions went unrecorded. In addition to works by and about Rayburn in Chapters 2 and 3, this bio-bibliography lists major archival sources where oral histories and letters involving Rayburn may be found.

It should be noted that the biographical sketch relies in part on D.B. Hardeman and Don Bacon's critically acclaimed and recently published biography of Rayburn, Rayburn: A Biography (1987). That book is an especially valuable source since it is based on years of personal interactions between Hardeman and Rayburn. Source materials, including transcripts of lengthy interviews with Rayburn, have not yet been made public. However, they will eventually be made available to scholars at the Sam Rayburn Library in Bonham, Texas.

Many of Rayburn's private papers prior to 1940 were lost when he exchanged offices with Joe Martin, a close friend of Rayburn who for many years was his Republican counterpart in the House of Representatives. Rayburn searched for these missing papers for several years as did staff members. A Capitol police officer, whose career was once saved by Rayburn, spent years after Rayburn's death trying to locate those papers. To

date, they have not been found. Rayburn concluded
eventually that they had been destroyed; however, it
may be that they will eventually be found in the maze
of storage areas in the Capitol. Should they ever be
found, they will prove a valuable resource for
historians since material from the Wilson
Administration through much of the Roosevelt
Administration is included.

The most useful information on Rayburn is currently on
file at the Sam Rayburn Library in Bonham, Texas. Many
of Rayburn´s papers from 1940-1961 and some pre-1940
materials are located there. Extensive news clippings
on Rayburn are also available from both national and
local newspapers. Additionally, approximately eighty
oral histories by friends and associates of Rayburn,
particularly those in his Congressional district and in
Texas, are available there.

Parenthetical numbers in Chapter 1 refer to the
numbered annotations in the bibliography. Complete
citations are listed there along with page numbers
where they are appropriate. Numbers in parentheses in
the index also refer to the numbered annotations; other
entry numbers refer to the appropriate pages in the
sketch.

Rayburn was one of the most influential of all American
Congressmen. He has become the prototype of the
effective leader of the House of Representatives. I
hope this bio-bibliography offers readers insight into
the man´s beliefs and character and some understanding
of the forces that influenced his thinking. I believe
that it can provide guidance to those wishing to
pursue additional studies of the man whom so many
simply called "Mr. Sam."

Acknowledgments

I am indebted to H.G. Dulaney, Director of the Sam
Rayburn Library, for his assistance with this research
on Sam Rayburn. H.G. has had a major role in
perpetuating the memory of Speaker Rayburn.

I am also indebted to Cynthia Keheley and to Marie
Walls for their help in preparing the manuscript.

Finally, thanks are due to the numerous associates of
Sam Rayburn who agreed to be interviewed for my
research. Transcripts of those interviews are on file
in the Sam Rayburn Library. I am also grateful for the
assistance provided by the archivists of the following
libraries: Alabama Department of Archives and History;
Carl Albert and Western History Collection, University
of Oklahoma; Dallas Historical Society; John F. Kennedy
Library; Harry S Truman Library; Dwight D. Eisenhower
Library; Lyndon B. Johnson Library; North Texas State
University Oral History Collection; Franklin D.
Roosevelt Library; The Joe T. Robinson papers in the
University of Arkansas Library Special Collections
Department; and East Texas State University.

Chronology

1882   January 6, born in Roane County, Tennessee.

1887   Farm purchased by Rayburn´s parents at Flag Springs, near Bonham, Texas.

1900   Enrolled Mayo College, Commerce, Texas.

1903   Graduated with a B.S. degree from Mayo College.

1906   Elected for the first of three two-year terms to the Texas House of Representatives.

1908   Admitted to the bar.

1911   Elected Speaker of the Texas House of Representatives.

1912   Elected for the first of twenty-five two-year terms to U.S. House of Representatives.

1921   Elected Chairman of the Democratic Caucus of the U.S. House of Representatives.

1927   Married and divorced Metze Jones of Valley View, Texas.

1931-   Chairman, Committee on Interstate and Foreign
1936   Commerce.

1937-   Majority Leader, U.S. House of Representatives.
1940

1940-   Speaker, U.S. House of Representatives.
1946

1947– Minority Leader, U.S. House of Representatives.
1948

1949– Speaker, U.S. House of Representatives.
1952

1953– Minority Leader, U.S. House of Representatives.
1954

1955– Speaker, U.S. House of Representatives.
1961

1961   November 16, died of cancer of the pancreas at
       Bonham, Texas.

SAM RAYBURN

1

Biographical Sketch

INTRODUCTION

The popular image of Sam Rayburn is that he was very powerful and very bald (137). Most people are aware that he was a major political force; however, they do not realize that he was in public life for over half a century and that he was one of the nation's most influential Congressmen for a quarter of a century. He was a protege of Joe Bailey and John Nance Garner and a mentor to Lyndon Johnson, Carl Albert, Hale Boggs, and Richard Bolling (040, 136). This quiet, reticent Texan (043), wielded the Speaker's gavel longer than anyone in American history and served as a U.S. representative during the administrations of eight presidents (025, 039, 084, 218). Loved by his constituents (018), respected by his fellow politicians (017), he has become in Texas and within the study of Congressional politics, a legendary figure.

Myths have developed surrounding Rayburn--that he was a bachelor (037); that he was lonely and unsociable (043); and that his greatest ambition was to serve in the U.S. House of Representatives and to be its Speaker (017). Yet, other Rayburn legends are not mythical--he was an unusually skilled politician (017), who was especially attentive to his constituents (018, 136); he was a powerful personality (017); and he was able to bridge the regional differences within the Democratic Party (065).

Rayburn was in essence a power broker with a strong pragmatic streak that allowed him vast ideological flexibility (021, 058). If he possessed a consistent ideology over his lengthy career, it was that of a populist (149). He was bonded to the land and to small farmers (153). Rayburn was dedicated to improving rural life and regulating those economic forces that burdened the lives of farmers (136). Like his close friends, President Harry Truman and Chief Justice Fred Vinson, he had little interest in accumulating personal wealth (029, 163). When he died, his estate included the family farm, some pastureland near Bonham, Texas, and about $15,000 in savings (216). That was part of the legend of Sam Rayburn that developed even during his lifetime: He was a man of rock-ribbed integrity who inspired trust (017). It was a valuable trait for one who continually bargained within the legislative process.

Rayburn wrote one of his sisters in 1922, "I would rather link my name indelibly with the living pulsing history of my country and not be forgotten entirely after while [sic] than to have anything else on Earth" (192). This sketch of the life of Sam Rayburn, a man who was so much a part of twentieth century Congressional history, suggests that he achieved his dream.

THE EARLY YEARS

An objective observer of Sam Rayburn as a youth would have offered a dim assessment of his prospects for becoming one of the nation's most famous and most effective members of Congress. He was born in 1882 in Roane County, Tennessee, and was the eighth of eleven children. His parents were small farmers who moved to northeast Texas near the town of Bonham in 1887. Corn farmers in Tennessee, they became cotton farmers in Texas (100).

Young Sam helped on the farm and became impressed with politics after hearing the speeches of Congressman and later Senator Joe Bailey (040). Bailey was both physically impressive and a dynamic speaker who evoked feelings of either love or hate among Texans (094, 099). Unusually vindictive, Bailey, for example, once boasted in a letter to Rayburn,

> My enemies have never made a more serious mistake than they are making now in attacking me upon the tariff question. My position is not only unassailable as a matter of logic and justice, but it is in strict accord with the time-honored principles of the Democratic Party.... I am really eager to get to Texas so that I can smite these people 'hip and thigh' (097).

Throughout his life, Bailey seemed to thrive on controversy. As a young politician, Bailey was a progressive Democrat. He was a free silver proponent, an advocate of free trade, and an anti-imperialist. He supported the regulation of railroads and was a strong proponent of the income tax. In what seems a contradiction of the views of his youth, he became the voice of extreme conservatism and opposed women's suffrage and prohibition. Although he was pragmatic from time to time, as he grew older, he became increasingly conservative and anti-progressive. Not careful in matters of finance and political ethics, he publicly defended ties between politicians and corporate interests. Eventually, he resigned from the U.S. Senate amid charges that he had accepted bribes from a company controlled by Standard Oil (094, 096, 099).

Young Sam Rayburn and his family were captivated by the dynamic Bailey, and Rayburn was to become a Bailey loyalist in his earliest years in politics. Rayburn described his early admiration for Bailey as beginning in 1894 when he was only twelve. Congressman Bailey was scheduled to speak in Bonham, and Rayburn rode for eleven miles upon the back of a mule in a heavy rain in order to hear Bailey. As he described the experience,

> I'd never been to Bonham since we bought the farm, and I was scared of all the rich townsfolk in their store-bought clothes. But I found a flap in the canvas, and I stuck there like glue while old Joe Bailey made his speech. He went on for two solid hours, and I scarcely drew a breath the whole time. I can still feel the water dripping down my neck. I slipped around to the entrance again when he was through, saw him come out, and ran after him five or six blocks until he got on a streetcar. Then I went home, wondering whether I'd ever be as big a man as Joe Bailey (211).

Rayburn described his excitement over the experience saying, "This Adonis of a man with a massive brain captured my imagination and became my model" (084, p. 8). It was said that after that experience, Rayburn's siblings would sneak near the barn and hear Rayburn giving political speeches to the farm animals (084).

That youthful enthusiasm for Bailey was less ebullient several years later due to Bailey's alleged corruption. In 1922, for example, Rayburn wrote to his brother-in-law, W.A. Thomas, "I am of the definite opinion that Bailey is badly fooled as he usually is in politics..." (193). However, his fondness for Bailey never completely waned. Even when Rayburn was Speaker, he wrote admiringly of Bailey, "I have never known a man or heard a man who had more power over an audience or was a greater public speaker than Joseph Weldon Bailey, and I have heard all the men ... Bourke Cochran, W.J. Bryan, Albert J. Beveridge, James A. Reed, William E. Borah and Winston Churchill" (205). Bailey's famed oratorical skills were at their peak when he endorsed conservative Democratic concepts such as states rights, limited government, and white supremacy (096).

As a poor farm boy, Rayburn experienced the hardships of rural America in the late nineteenth and early twentieth century (190). Later as an influential Congressman deeply involved in programs aimed at the economic development of rural America, he was to claim that his memories of the privations of farm life led him to battle for programs such as rural electrification, farm-to-market roads, public power, and soil conservation, (039, 106, 136, 155). He frequently recalled his rural upbringing in his political speeches and stressed the hardships of farm life. After the New Deal, he especially stressed the difficulties of farm life during the Great Depression. He would then mention the many programs he had supported which benefited the farmer. Such themes were so routine in his speeches within the district that one of his sisters argued that they had been overdone. To that Rayburn claimed that he would keep repeating those things because he never wanted people to forget how hard farm life was before the New Deal (040). Another associate told him that the district was changing and that his speeches needed updating because many people could not remember the Great Depression, life without electricity, or four cent a pound cotton. Rayburn promised that friend that he would try to update his appeals, but he never did so (135). A typical post-New Deal speech by Rayburn would remind constituents of Republican hard times and Democratic good ones:

> I can remember four and one half cent cotton.
> I sold one thousand bushels of oats out here
> one year for ninety dollars. If I had it now
> I could get one thousand dollars for it. We
> sold our cotton at twenty-two and one half a
> bale. Now we can get a hundred and fifty or
> more. Cotton seed [sic] were burned in those
> days. They are very valuable now because we
> do not have too much oil of any kind. Cattle

hogs and oil were selling at a price that it gave nobody a buying power (202).

Although interested in politics from childhood, Rayburn first attended college to become a teacher. With money saved by his father and supporting himself with odd jobs, he attended Mayo College in Commerce, Texas. Rayburn was to have a fondness for Professor Mayo and his college for the remainder of his life. In 1960, he wrote,

> If a student had any zeal, any ambition, Professor Mayo was able to inspire him to work hard and to succeed.... In addition, Professor Mayo made it possible for hundreds and hundreds of young people to go to college who could not have afforded to attend another institution.... If it hadn´t been for Mayo´s College, his credit system, and his inspiration, I don´t know where I´d be today. Professor Mayo instilled in me the importance of a man´s having an objective in life, of the need to have a program and to bend every energy to it (212, p. 25).

In the 1940s, Rayburn began a tense relationship with East Texas State Teachers College, formerly Mayo College. Its president, James Gee, was a conservative who was anti-New Deal and anti-Rayburn. He supported Rayburn´s political opponents and claimed Rayburn wanted to stack the faculty with political supporters (002, 136, 141, 142, 204). Even after Rayburn´s death, Gee had to be pressured by such Rayburn friends as Congressman Ray Roberts, Rayburn´s successor as Fourth District Congressman, to refer to the student union at the college by its proper name, the Sam Rayburn Student Union (151).

He taught briefly in rural schools although he soon ran for the Texas House of Representatives. Rayburn traveled to the communities in the district with his opponent, meeting people and giving speeches at every opportunity (039).

Rayburn won his first political race and then won two additional races for the Texas House of Representatives. He was later to describe himself as very conservative during those early years and also as very much under the influence of Joe Bailey (040). He was anti-women´s suffrage; however, he did support programs popular with progressives such as prohibition (098, 136). During those years, the Texas House of Representatives had a tradition of loose political ethics, yet Rayburn developed a reputation for integrity during that time which he maintained throughout a long political career. It was said that he was a man for whom a lobbyist could not even buy a meal (017).

In his first term as a state representative, he authored two bills: one guaranteed deposits in state banks; the other, co-authored by his friend Bouna Ridgway, required automobiles to have a bell and light, set the speed limit for automobiles within cities at eight miles per hour, and gave horses and carriages right of way over cars (025).

He took advantage of the opportunity to attend The University of Texas Law School while he was in the state legislature and he was admitted to the bar. However, he never had an extensive legal practice and refused legal fees from corporations that had legislative business (084). He passed the bar in 1908, but he claimed he was so active in politics that he never had time to develop a significant legal practice. After he was elected to the U.S. Congress in 1912, claimed Rayburn, "I had no time whatever to devote to law and, therefore, never practiced much. I am glad, however, that I got as much of the background as I did. I never expected to follow the law if I could remain in politics which was my burning ambition all my life" (214). Speaking of his refusal to accept fees from public service corporations, he claimed in a political speech in 1912,

> When I became a member of the law firm of Steger, Thurmond and Rayburn, Messrs. Thurmond and Steger were representing the Santa Fe Railroad Company, receiving pay monthly. When the first check came after I entered the firm, Mr. Thurmond brought to my desk one-third of the amount of the check, explaining what it was for. I said to him that I was a member of the Legislature, representing the people of Fannin County, and that my experience had taught me that men who represent the people should be as far removed as possible from concerns whose interests he was liable to be called on to legislate concerning, and that on that ground I would not accept a dollar of the railroad's money... (187).

Law for Rayburn was not a vocation or even a hobby; rather, it seemed to provide him with a sense of security should he fail in his dreams for a lifelong political career.

In his second term, Speaker A. M. Kennedy's leadership was challenged on the grounds that he had improperly spent money for furniture and for wages for a House employee. Rayburn, perceiving the attack on Kennedy as due to Kennedy's proposals to investigate the state's prison system and method of schoolbook selection, led the fight to defend the Speaker. That support for Kennedy, although unsuccessful in saving the Texas Speakership for him, suggested to other members of the House that Rayburn should be considered for the Speakership. It was not to happen during Rayburn's second term, although he chaired two House committees that term and served on four others. After he was elected to his third term as a Texas legislator, he successfully ran for Speaker of the Texas House of Representatives. Although one writer has claimed that Rayburn was elected Speaker because of the respect for him by other legislators (017), both his close ties with Joe Bailey, who was then a political power in Texas politics, and the support of former Speaker Kennedy played a large part in Rayburn being chosen as Speaker. It was a thrilling experience for Rayburn. Accounts indicate that the normally reticent young man yelled with a whoop when it was announced that he had won the Speakership (025, 039, 084). Late in his life, he confessed to a political associate who had also been Speaker of the Texas House of Representatives, that the job was the most enjoyable he had ever held (161). He also admitted that during those years he was only able to get through the legislative session "by God, by desperation and by ignorance" (084, p. 23)

During the last few years of the nineteenth century and the early years of the twentieth, there was a strong progressive movement in Texas. The House during Rayburn's term as Speaker tended to reflect that progressivism. Contrary to Rayburn's claim that he had been quite conservative as a young man (040), as Speaker, Rayburn supported public school improvements, regulation of utilities, interest payments by banks on state deposits, limitations on working hours for women, and pure food standards (039).

The Speakership provided the opportunity for Rayburn to run for the U.S. House of Representatives. The state legislature redistricted while Rayburn was Speaker and he was able to influence the drawing of new district boundaries. His old friend Joe Bailey had resigned from the U.S. Senate amid scandal, and the Congressman from the Congressional district in which Rayburn lived, Choice Randell, chose to be a candidate for the Senate. Rayburn became a candidate for the U. S. House seat while making sure that a key likely

opponent's home county would not be within the
Congressional district.   Nevertheless, it was not an
easy race for Rayburn.   There were seven candidates in
the Democratic primary.   The opposition included two
influential local politicians--a state senator from
McKinney in Collin County and a state district judge
from Sherman in Grayson County.   In those days, the
Republican Party did not mount candidates and so
victory in the Democratic primary was tantamount to
election.   Rayburn campaigned in a Model-T Ford that he
bought for the occasion, and he relied heavily upon a
volunteer campaign committee, led by such community
influentials as his law partner, the editor of the
Bonham paper, and the presiding elder of the Methodist
Church in Bonham.   His campaign committee organized
motorcades   of   Rayburn   supporters   who   traveled
throughout the district spreading Rayburn's name.
Rayburn himself gave numerous speeches and in those
speeches he announced his support for tariffs for
revenue only, for the right of labor to organize, for
an income tax and an inheritance tax, and for popular
election of the President (025, 039, 084).   There was
nothing unique or original about Rayburn's positions;
such positions were fairly typical for populists in
that day. It was a narrow victory for Rayburn who won
the primary with only a plurality of 23% of the 21,336
votes cast.   In those days there was no runoff primary,
and so a plurality was all that was necessary for
victory (102).

THE NEW FREEDOM

The career of Sam Rayburn in the U.S. Congress was
to span nearly 49 years.   Beginning with the advent of
Woodrow Wilson's New Freedom, it extended through the
administrations of Warren Harding, Calvin Coolidge,
Herbert Hoover, Franklin Roosevelt, Harry Truman,
Dwight Eisenhower, and the first year of John Kennedy's
New Frontier.   Never was Sam Rayburn to be defeated in
25 Congressional elections.   Indeed, in all regular
elections he was unopposed, although he frequently
faced Democratic primary opposition, some of which was
strong opposition.   He faced Democratic Party primary
opposition in 18 elections.   In his first race in 1912,
he won election to the House of Representatives with
only a plurality of 23% of the primary vote, and he had
primary election victory margins of 5% or less in 1916,
1922, 1930, 1932, and 1944 (045, 136).   The frequent
number of primary battles and the six close races made
Rayburn extremely sensitive to providing service to his
district (002).

When Rayburn went to Washington in 1913, his friendship with Joe Bailey continued (053). It was Bailey who sponsored Rayburn for admission to practice before the U.S. Supreme Court (103). It was also the tie to Bailey which provided a bond with John Nance Garner, a fellow Texan who was a major influence upon Rayburn's career. Garner was an attorney, a banker, and was involved in land speculation in the Rio Grande Valley. Prior to being elected to Congress, he had served as a county judge and had been in the state legislature. Garner had been a Bailey ally when he served in the Texas legislature. Closely allied to both Bailey and the notorious South Texas political boss, Jim Wells, he proved to be a pragmatic politician who supported Bailey, states' rights, white supremacy and such progressive reforms as state anti-trust laws, insurance industry regulation, and tax reform. Having sponsored legislation desired by Jim Wells while he was in the Texas legislature, he became Wells' candidate for Congress and was elected to the U.S. House of Representatives in 1902. After being elected to the House, Garner cooperated with the Democratic leadership and became a close associate of Democratic leader Champ Clark, who appointed him party whip in 1909. With the election of 1910, the Democrats gained control of the House. Garner retained his position as whip and served on a three-member committee which distributed House patronage. In 1913, he gained membership on the Ways and Means Committee due to the departure of Choice Randell, Rayburn's predecessor in Congress (016, 049, 088, 096). One of the major committees of the House, the Democratic members of the Ways and Means Committee had additional influence over the members of their party since they made Democratic committee assignments. Garner aided Rayburn in obtaining a seat on the Interstate and Foreign Commerce Committee. That committee was one of the most important committees of the House. It had jurisdiction over legislation which involved the Commerce Clause of the Constitution. The only committee on which Rayburn served during his lengthy Congressional career, he became its chairman in 1931. It was as its chairman during the New Deal that he first developed a reputation as a master legislator (039).

No doubt Rayburn was grateful to Garner for his help. The friendship which developed between the two of them paved the way for Rayburn's advancement to Congressional leadership. As Garner moved to the Democratic leadership, then to the Speakership, to the status of Presidential contender in 1932, and finally to the Vice Presidency, Rayburn's influence in Congress increased as well until the trusted Garner lieutenant became himself a mentor of more junior Congressmen (040, 126).

The success of the Garner-Rayburn partnership was in the future, however. Rayburn in the early years of the Wilson Administration was merely a newcomer with some impressive state legislative experience. He was also totally dedicated to political life and took rapidly to learning about the House of Representatives. Rayburn quickly gained a reputation on his committee as a hard worker with primary interests in the area of railroad regulation. In those early years, however, he proved to be somewhat impetuous. He did not follow the tradition of remaining quiet during his first term, and he chose to give his maiden speech at an early point in the Congressional session. That speech was on the tariff. It expressed opposition to the protective tariff, adoration of President Wilson, and opposition to the Republican Party (017, 039, 188). During this term, he visited the Panama Canal. Panama City he found to be "very old looking ... very dirty and filled with negroes" (189). It was one of only two or three trips that he ever took outside the United States--the other trips were only brief visits to Mexico (038). Upon returning to Washington from Panama, he urged repeal of a law establishing toll free passage of American vessels through the Canal. Most importantly, during those first months in Washington, he wrote a bill, modeled on a bill passed in Texas during Governor Jim Hogg's administration, which regulated stock and bond issuances of state railroads. Rayburn's bill gave the Interstate Commerce Commission regulatory power over the issuance of stocks and bonds of interstate railroads. Louis Brandeis, coordinating anti-trust legislation for the Wilson Administration, decided to make the Rayburn Railroad Stock and Bond Bill a major part of Wilson's New Freedom anti-trust proposals. Other parts of Wilson's anti-trust package included creation of the Federal Trade Commission with authority to investigate and end unfair trade practices and the Clayton Anti-Trust Bill which made illegal certain restraints of trade such as price fixing, insider contracts, and some corporate combinations. Rayburn's bill passed the House, but, prior to passage by the Senate, the Wilson Administration withdrew its support for the bill. Initially, Brandeis began to feel doubts about the constitutionality of the legislation, then he concluded that the public might see ICC approval of a railroad stock or bond issuance as a guarantee of the issuance by the U.S. government. Wilson began to back away from the bill when war in Europe broke out in August, 1914. The withdrawal of support by the Administration, coupled with opposition from states' rights oriented senators who saw the bill as an expansion of federal power, killed Rayburn's bill. Although Rayburn reintroduced the bill the following year, Wilson refused to endorse it, and Rayburn personally met with the President, became angry with Wilson, and abruptly cut off his meeting with the President (017, 025, 039, 084, 101).

It was his first major legislative failure as a Congressman. Nevertheless, Rayburn managed to recover from that defeat rapidly enough to succeed in other legislative matters during the Wilson years. He successfully sponsored legislation which made the initial rail carrier responsible for goods damaged in transit and provided that the carrier would have full liability. He also was involved in both committee work and in the House chamber on the Adamson Act which provided a 20% increase in pay for railroad workers and which provided for an eight-hour day for those workers. With the outbreak of World War I, he became a dedicated supporter of the Wilson Administration and of war-related measures. Of special note was his sponsorship of the War Risk Insurance Bill which provided for $10,000 in life insurance to servicemen (025, 039, 084).

Rayburn seemed to recognize that he needed seasoning as a Congressman and that he was poorly educated. It became his practice to seek the counsel of more senior representatives. Speaker Champ Clark, for example, suggested that he needed to read more, particularly biographies, and he even gave Rayburn a list of suggested readings. Throughout the remainder of his life, Rayburn remained a voracious reader of political biographies (025). Rayburn also developed close friendships with men who would one day wield great power, such as Congressman Cordell Hull (055), and Congressman Alben Barkley (004). Most important, was the friendship with Garner.

John Nance Garner represented the Rio Grande Valley of Texas. He was a rugged man with a red face and enormous white bushy eyebrows. He enjoyed cigars, whisky, poker, and politics--not necessarily in that order. Very bright, hot-tempered, and possessing vast parliamentary knowledge, his was a strong personality which could be quite intimidating (016, 049, 054, 088, 123). He enjoyed testing the strength of other men's characters. One associate claimed that Garner enjoyed testing other Congressmen's mettle by inviting them for a drink. He would pour them a large glass of bad whisky, and, if they drank and did not complain, he knew he could control them (175). He was a notoriously thrifty man whose carefulness with money was legendary and who employed his wife as his Congressional secretary. This secretive, not very likeable man, became Rayburn's new political mentor after the disgrace of Joe Bailey (011).

Garner and the Republican Speaker Nicholas Longworth were strong personal friends. After each day's Congressional session, they would retreat to a private room in the Capitol for drinks and political conversation. As Garner's regular guest, Rayburn gained entry into some of the best informed political conversation in the Capitol, as well as having access to the most influential members of the House. Rayburn in those early years seemed to be in awe of John Garner and saw him as "a man of rare intelligence and industry" (039, p. 71). Garner, on the other hand, seemed to view Rayburn as a valuable, if somewhat shy, lieutenant. He told a mutual friend that Rayburn had great ability, but that he would have to overcome his shyness (023). Shyness was not one of Garner's qualities. He was a rough man with a forceful personality (084), and he was an avid practitioner of pork barrel politics. His comment, "Every time one of those Yankees gets a ham, I'm going to do my best to get a hog" (096, p. 122), has become famous.

Garner treated people roughly and Rayburn was no exception. Martin Dies, longtime conservative Texas Congressman, recalled,

> He [Garner] was tough, wiry, and he taught politics to Sam Rayburn. Sam Rayburn was his boy Friday, and John Garner was very rough with his subordinates and very rough with Sam. I heard him dress Sam down one time before some eight or nine members and I don't think I could have taken it, perhaps I could, but I don't think I could have. But, at any rate, he trained Sam Rayburn--was responsible for Sam's advancement (111).

During the Wilson Administration, Rayburn was learning about the House, meeting influential politicians, working conscientiously on his committee, and having some impact on policy. Yet his lack of cooperation with regard to the railroad stock and bond regulation legislation had angered Wilson. In 1916, Rayburn was challenged in the Democratic primary by Andrew Randell, the son of the former Congressman from the area, Choice Randell. Both men ran on strong pro-Wilson platforms and both claimed the support of Woodrow Wilson. When Rayburn claimed Wilson's endorsement, Randell produced a letter from Wilson which was favorable to Randell and which denied the endorsement of Rayburn. Randell was Princeton educated and had been a former student of Wilson. It was likely that his upper-class education and well-to-do background benefited Rayburn, the Mayo College educated farmer's son, in the primary. Rayburn always was able to maintain a personal identification with the small farmer constituency that was the Fourth Congressional District. With 55% of the votes in the Democratic primary, he was able to survive the first of several major challenges to his incumbency (136).

REPUBLICAN CONTROL: HARDING THROUGH HOOVER

With the election of a Republican controlled House of Representatives in 1918 and President Warren G. Harding in 1920, Rayburn's influence over policy was vastly reduced. The Republican dominance of the White House and Congress did not end until the Great Depression broke the Republican Party's hold over the Capitol. During that decade, it is as if Rayburn shrank from the political scene with only moments when he was visible to outside Congressional observers. He retained his committee, his friendships, his reputation for integrity and conscientiousness, and his alliance with Garner, but he was a member of a minority party without leadership responsibility (051).

In the House of Representatives, the Republican Party outnumbered the Democratic Party by nearly three to one. Harding's election had brought the defeat of so many senior Democrats that Rayburn was regarded as a senior Congressman, but he had virtually no influence over Administration policy. He was elected by his fellow Democratic Congressmen as Chairman of the Democratic Caucus. In the same Congress his only legislative efforts were the introduction of nine bills to donate Confederate cannons to nine communities in his district. Perhaps because he was elected to chair the Caucus, he saw himself as a leader of the party and he became a very partisan critic of the Republican Party (191). He also began to move to the right of his earlier progressive positions, reflecting either the change in the temper of the country or considering a move to the U.S. Senate from Texas to replace the ailing Senator Charles Culbertson (025, 039, 084).

Many of his political attitudes reflected the mainstream of Southern Democratic politics. His father was a Confederate Civil War veteran, and the Civil War was not forgotten by Rayburn. Throughout his life, he maintained a strong admiration for Robert E. Lee and he held strong Southern loyalties. In his early years in politics, he sometimes gave speeches which reeked of white supremacist ideology. Loyalty to the Democratic Party, the party of the South, was an important value for him. As was fairly typical of rural Southern representatives, he was in favor of free trade, favored prohibition, and had concerns about women's suffrage (025, 136, 147, 196).

At home in 1922, he faced a major primary challenge by state senator Ed Westbrook. Denison, Texas, was in his district and was the site of the Katy Railroad locomotive repair shops. As a result, the railroad unions held great sway. Rayburn supported the postwar return of the railroads to private control; while the unions supported continued government control. The struggle over control of the railroads was a nationwide one that led to a national railroad strike and to great violence. The Denison strike was also violent and, on one occasion when Rayburn spoke there, he had to be protected by Texas Rangers (136). The American Federation of Labor labeled Rayburn as "the workingman's enemy" and noted that in addition to his opposition to continued federal operation of the railroads he had opposed the $3 a day minimum wage, opposed the child labor law, and opposed the seven-hour day for government employees. Interestingly, the railroads also opposed Rayburn due to his stock and bond bill and his liability bill for goods damaged in transit. Rayburn was also opposed by the Ku Klux Klan which had gained such influence in Texas that its candidate, Earle B. Mayfield, won the Democratic primary for U.S. Senator from Texas. Even farmers who were associated with the Farmer-Labor Union opposed Rayburn. They blamed those in political power for low farm prices that had resulted from the Harding Administration's deflation policies. Rayburn won that primary with 52% of the votes. His margin of victory was only 1,254 votes; so close was his victory that in the early hours of the vote count he blurted, "I've lost this race" (084, p. 72). His position with the railroad unions in the district remained especially tenuous until the Roosevelt era when his support of the New Deal endeared him to his district's unions (058).

Rayburn married in 1927. He was 45 years old when he married Metze Jones. She was only 27 years old and was the sister of his close friend, Congressman Marvin Jones of Amarillo (061). Rayburn at this stage in his life had just lost his mother through death. He had been very close to his mother, and it seems likely that the marriage was an effort to reach for companionship during a time of great personal sadness. Contrary to popular mythology, Rayburn did have a social life and did enjoy the company of women. It appears that he had over the course of his life sexual relationships with several women (039, 068). There were long-term affairs with a very small number of women and one long-term affair, involving the widow of a cabinet member in the Wilson Administration, that seemed to border on marriage. That woman had only a small amount of money; so Rayburn arranged for her to receive a small federal patronage job in order to provide her with an adequate income (067). Although he was short and bald, he exuded masculinity and was quite popular with women. However, the marriage to Metze failed after less than three months. Neither Metze nor Rayburn ever spoke of the reasons for the divorce, and the divorce documents have disappeared from the Fannin County Courthouse. One story is that by the time of their marriage, Rayburn was a heavy drinker and that Metze was offended by the drinking and by the social life of Washington, which was no doubt quite different from that of her home in Valley View, Texas. It was said that they quarreled publicly over Rayburn´s drinking at a party given by another Congressman and that Metze left Washington for Texas shortly thereafter (025, 039, 084, 129, 136). Whatever the reason, the divorce hurt Rayburn immensely. Many years later, during a party he emotionally defended Adlai Stevenson who was being criticized for being divorced. Rayburn said that divorce should not be held against a person since it was often no fault of his own. It was claimed by one person who attended the party that Rayburn was so emotional that he must have been thinking about his own divorce (067). He once told a friend that his divorce had hurt him so badly that he would never marry again (067). Late in his life, he was to express deep regrets that he had never had a child. Yet, he never expressed bitterness toward Metze. When she remarried and a son had polio, he used his influence to get the child admitted to the Warm Springs Foundation (084). When Rayburn was dying, he asked Marvin Jones about Metze and asked to see her (052).

The marriage was brief and there was no scandal associated with the divorce. As a result, it was mostly forgotten, and Rayburn began to describe himself and to be described as a bachelor (037). Due to his reticent personality, relatively little was known about his personal life, and it was assumed that he had none. He did tend to dislike many social occasions. He also spent much time alone in his apartment in Washington. Additionally, he loved politics and the House of Representatives and seemed lonely and uncomfortable when he was not involved with politics (043).   However, he did attend parties and enjoyed socializing with friends.   He also attended events such as White House dinners and some embassy parties.   He even hosted small dinners in his apartment from time to time.   Rayburn was in love with politics; however, he was not the recluse with neither nonpolitical nor female companionship that has sometimes been suggested (050, 066, 093).

There must have seemed no end to Republican control of Congress and the White House for the ambitious Sam Rayburn of the 1920s.   In 1927 Rayburn became the most senior Democrat on the Interstate and Foreign Commerce Committee; however, there seemed to be little prospect that the Republicans would soon lose power in the House of Representatives and provide the opportunity for Rayburn to chair the committee.

The 1928 Presidential campaign saw the Democratic Party test the loyalty of its Southern members with the nomination of Al Smith of New York for the Presidency. Smith was a Tammany Hall Democrat, antiprohibition, and a Catholic.   For many in the conservative South, it was too great a test of party loyalty (089).   A poem from a church bulletin found in the files of Smith's vice presidential running mate, Senator Joe Robinson, provides one indication of the extent of that bigotry,

> Alcohol Al for president;
> I stand for whiskey and bad government;
> My platform is wet and I am too,
> And I get my votes from Catholic and Jew.
> The ignorant wop and the gangster too,
> Are the trash I expect to carry me thru [sic],
> And when I land in the White House chair,
> They can be hanged for all I care.
> I'll rule the people and the pope will rule me,
> And the people's rights you will never see,
> And the Protestant heretics who vote for me,
> I'll reduce to adject [sic] slavery.
> I'll take down the flag from the public schools,
> And put up the cross for the ignorant fools,
> The Bible in the school shall not be read,
> But instead we'll say masses for the dead.
> And the flag you love shall be put down,
> And put up instead the papal crown;
> Then the pope of Rome shall rule the homes
> And bring back the glory that once was
> Rome's...(095).

Many Texans found it impossible to vote for Smith. Religious bigotry was especially prevalent in Texas, and a pro-Hoover movement among nominal Democrats gained support. In spite of the strong opposition to Smith in Northeast Texas and widespread bolting of the party by Texas Democratic officeholders, Rayburn remained loyal to the Democratic ticket and campaigned for Smith (046). At times in campaigning for Smith, Rayburn used bigotry to fight bigotry. When, for example, Smith was accused of being pro-Negro, Rayburn claimed that Herbert Hoover integrated the rest rooms in the Commerce Department during the time he was its secretary. He also appealed to traditional Texas loyalty to the Democratic Party claiming,

> As long as I honor the memory of the Confederate dead, and revere the gallant devotion of my Confederate father to our Southland, I will never vote for electors of a Party which sent the carpetbagger and the scalawag to the prostrate South with saber and sword (196).

Many years later, when John Kennedy was a candidate for the Democratic Presidential nomination, Rayburn was accused of opposing Kennedy because of personal hostility to Catholicism (182). His subsequent support of Kennedy once he received the Presidential nomination and his arguments against the religious bigotry evidenced in that Presidential campaign indicate that the alternative interpretation of Rayburn´s views about Catholicism is valid (039, 136, 213, 215). Rayburn had seen the religious issue at its worst in the 1928 campaign. As he saw it, Kennedy was going to be subjected to the same attacks over his religion in 1960 and, like Smith, he would be defeated. As a result, he did not oppose Catholicism; he felt instead that a Catholic was unelectable (039, 136).

By 1930, the Great Depression had dealt Herbert Hoover and the Republican Party a cruel hand. It was clear that the Democrats finally had a chance to return to power. They gained control of the Congress as a result of the 1930 elections and in the House of Representatives, John Nance Garner became the Speaker. Rayburn, by this time in Congress for seventeen years, gained the chairmanship of the Interstate and Foreign Commerce Committee.

THE NEW DEAL

After the 1930 elections, it was clear that a Democrat could capture the White House in 1932. Garner, as Speaker of the House, was one of the

nation's most visible Democrats. Thus began the Garner
for President movement.   Rayburn was chosen to be
Garner's campaign manager. He did not feel that Garner
had a strong chance for the nomination. For one thing,
Garner was a Southerner, and it was unlikely that a
Southerner could win a national election. Memories of
the Civil War were too fresh, and politicians from the
South tended to be too extreme on the race question to
capture sufficient northern votes.   However, there was
no certain winner at the Democratic convention, and
thus Garner might win as a compromise candidate (197).

Soon it became clear that Franklin Roosevelt was the
front runner.   FDR needed two-thirds of the votes of
the delegates at the Democratic convention and, if he
was unsuccessful, Rayburn felt Garner might have a
chance. When the Democratic convention met, Roosevelt
was the front runner, but he lacked two-thirds of the
votes.   Acting with Garner's proxy, Rayburn released
the Texas delegates to vote for Roosevelt which assured
him the nomination (113, 114, 200). Rayburn has been
heavily criticized for this action. It has been argued
that, if Garner had participated in the "Stop
Roosevelt" movement, Roosevelt would have been denied
the nomination and Garner would have been the nominee
(021).   Rayburn and Garner refused to work to stop
Roosevelt because they did not want a deadlocked
convention such as occurred in 1924 when John W. Davis
was nominated after more than one hundred ballots
(003). Both men were party loyalists who did not want
to risk losing a likely Democratic victory with a badly
divided and embittered Democratic Party.

In exchange for being granted the nomination,
Roosevelt chose Garner to be his vice-presidential
running mate. Burns has argued that another part of
the Roosevelt-Garner agreement was that Rayburn would
have Roosevelt's support for the House leadership.
Burns provides no support for this statement (107),
although it is clear that Rayburn desired the
Speakership. He claimed that achieving the Speakership
had been his ambition since he was a boy (025). Such a
claim seems questionable given the limited visibility
of the office and the typical dreams of small boys.
Nevertheless, Rayburn's claim does suggest that he had
a long term desire for the office. At an earlier time,
he did not have the stature or the seniority to
seriously seek the office. By the early 1930s, he had
been in Congress for two decades, was chairman of a
major committee, and was well connected with the
Roosevelt Administration.   His ambition to become
Speaker was then taken seriously.

When Garner relinquished the Speakership for the vice-presidency in 1933, Rayburn evidenced his first efforts to attain the Speakership. Although he was not an active candidate, he maintained himself as an available one. He was disadvantaged in his desire to be Speaker because of a feeling held by many members of Congress that Texans, with the vice-presidency and a number of committee chairmanships, already held too much power (108). Ultimately, along with the other Garner allies, he supported John McDuffie of Alabama for the Speakership, only to see him defeated by a coalition that made Henry Rainey of Illinois the Speaker and Joseph Byrns of Tennessee the majority leader (044, 134). Rainey died in August, 1934, and Rayburn again was a candidate for Speaker. This time he had the initial support of Garner, although it was later withdrawn either because Rayburn´s strength was uncertain or because Majority Leader Byrns threatened to oppose Garner´s renomination for the vice presidency in 1936 (108). Byrns offered Rayburn the floor leadership position to get him out of the race, but Rayburn refused. There were personal tensions between the two men, and, rather than accept the number two position under Byrns, Rayburn chose to continue chairing the Interstate and Foreign Commerce Committee (019). Rayburn´s friend and fellow Garner ally William Bankhead became the floor leader.

Joseph Byrns died in June, 1936. Bankhead suffered from severe heart disease which made it uncertain whether he would run for the Speakership. Even if he did so, his health made it clear that his tenure would be brief. With Bankhead running for Speaker, Rayburn was a candidate for floor leader. Although he had not been favorably disposed toward the floor leader´s job in the past, he knew it was the stepping stone to the Speakership and Bankhead, unlike Byrns, was a close friend with whom Rayburn had an excellent working relationship (108, 198).

Where were other candidates for the leadership as well, the most notable was John O´Connor of New York. O´Connor was chairman of the House Committee on Rules. O´Connor, like Rayburn, had his hopes for the leadership defeated in earlier years. Like Rayburn, he was chairman of a powerful committee. Unlike Rayburn, he was a Northerner, was a difficult personality, and was not considered loyal to Roosevelt (062, 104, 127).

Much of the race between the two men boiled down to an argument over regional balance in the House leadership and over which candidate had the support of Franklin Roosevelt. Rayburn was hindered by the large number of House committees that were chaired by Texans, by the vice-president being a Texan, and by Bankhead being a Southerner. His supporters argued that regional concerns should not determine a race as important as the floor leadership, but regional balance had traditionally been a major concern within the Democratic Party. Roosevelt would not directly interfere with the operation of the House by publicly endorsing a candidate for the speakership. There were, however, important signals that the administration preferred Rayburn. Vice President Garner publicly endorsed Rayburn, and state delegations such as Louisiana and Pennsylvania endorsed Rayburn. Louisiana officials, in the wake of Huey Long's assassination, were known to be seeking the friendship of the Roosevelt Administration. After Garner visited New Orleans, the delegation unexpectedly endorsed Rayburn even though some Louisiana Congressmen had previously promised their support to O'Connor. Pennsylvania's delegation, at the urging of the Democratic boss, Joseph Guffey, a Roosevelt stalwart, endorsed Rayburn as well (108).

With such signals of administration support, a feeling that O'Connor was too quarrelsome, and a strong and active campaign for the leadership by Rayburn, it was only necessary to break down the regional balance concerns for Rayburn to win. John McCormack, like O'Connor, a northern, Irish-Catholic, endorsed Rayburn and claimed loyalty to Roosevelt was far more important than regional concerns. McCormack had been an ally of Garner and was indebted to Rayburn for his help in securing McCormack a position on the Ways and Means Committee. His endorsement brought ten other New England Congressmen into the Rayburn camp (115). On January 4, 1937, Rayburn won the leadership position by a vote of 184-127 (108).

It was his last battle for leadership. When Bankhead died on September 15, 1940, Rayburn was chosen Speaker without Democratic opposition. He continued to be unopposed in the Democratic Caucus for every Speakership election thereafter until his death in 1961. With his rise to the Speakership, John McCormack, his loyal ally in the leadership race, became the majority leader. McCormack's selection as majority leader reinstituted the practice of regional balance in the Democratic leadership. After 27 years in the House, Rayburn achieved his ambition.

Although it is not widely remembered today, some of Rayburn's greatest legislative accomplishments occurred prior to gaining a position of leadership in the House.

As chairman of the Interstate and Foreign Commerce Committee, he made a reputation as a legislative master and his committee handled some of the most controversial bills of Roosevelt's first term (124, 129).

Less than one month after Roosevelt's inauguration, Rayburn introduced the administration's draft of a bill providing for federal supervision of investment securities which were sold in interstate commerce. The bill, which had been referred to Rayburn's committee, was a response to the need for public protection in the securities markets. The initial draft of the legislation was poorly written and Rayburn lacked expertise to improve the proposal. He had only owned stock once and had sold his $1,000 investment after worrying that it would pose a conflict of interest for him. He had never seen Wall Street and had never studied the financial pages. With help from James Landis, Thomas Corcoran, and Benjamin Cohen, he was able to design legislation which provided for disclosure in the sale of securities, and it was the Rayburn version of the legislation that was ultimately signed by the President on May 27, 1933 (039, 042).

The Interstate and Foreign Commerce Committee had been investigating railroad holding companies since 1931. In 1933, the investigation led to the passage of the Emergency Railroad Transportation Act. That legislation brought railroad holding companies under the jurisdiction of the Interstate Commerce Commission (039).

In 1934, the administration moved to regulate the stock exchanges themselves. Again working with Landis, Cohen, and Corcoran, Rayburn handled the bill in the House. Wall Street unleashed a strong propaganda campaign against the bill, but there was widespread public support for regulation of the exchanges in the face of securities abuses which had occurred. The Securities and Exchange Commission was created and stock exchanges were subject to regulation (026, 039).

Before the end of 1934, Rayburn's committee proposed and Rayburn floor managed the administration's plan to regulate the communication's industry. The result was that the Federal Communications Commission was created. Although much controversy later was to surround the bill's ban on wiretapping, Rayburn's regret was not over that provision, but rather that the bill had not forbidden the ownership of radio stations by newspapers (039).

As important as these bills were, his toughest legislative battle as committee chairman was the fight in 1935 over the breakup of the giant utility holding companies. The holding companies allowed bankers, large investors, and speculators to control the operating utility companies and to extract profits from those operating companies. In some cases, holding company would be piled upon holding company for several levels, all of them extracting profits from the operating companies. Sometimes the operating companies were also forced to buy services and materials from the parent companies at exorbitant rates which added to operating companies´ costs and to the consumer costs of utilities. Added to this was manipulation of utility stock prices and sale of those stocks to the public at inflated prices. Working with Corcoran and Cohen as his legislative draftsmen and technical experts and with Senator Burton Wheeler as the Senate sponsor, Rayburn introduced legislation calling for the abolition of utility holding companies. It was called the "death sentence" provision for holding companies (039, 092, 199).

It was a bill which began as one of Rayburn´s greatest frustrations. He knew that his support of the death sentence provision had caused the utility lobby to mark him for defeat. Additionally, he lost control of his committee over the provision, found Chairman John O´Connor and the House Committee on Rules to be uncooperative in granting his request for a record vote on the death sentence provision, and saw the provision defeated on the floor of the House. During this time he worried, lost sleep, and his unfriendly relationship with Speaker Joseph Byrns deteriorated even further (039).

The death sentence had cleared the Senate, however, and so victory was still possible with the bill that would be produced in the House-Senate conference. Prior to that conference, Senator Hugo Black conducted an investigation of the lobbying activities of the utility industry during the debate over the death sentence, and the gross lobbying improprieties made national headlines. Nevertheless, when Rayburn attempted to get the House to instruct its conferees to vote for the death sentence provision, he was defeated overwhelmingly. The investigation by Senator Black continued, and the revelations became even more embarrassing to the utility industry. The result was that Rayburn went before the House and asked them to instruct the conferees to accept a utility holding company death sentence compromise which had been developed by Senator Alben Barkley. The death sentence would have eliminated all holding companies beyond the first degree by 1942. Barkley's compromise would allow the Securities and Exchange Commission to make exceptions to the death sentence. This time the House voted with Rayburn, and the conferees were instructed to accept the Barkley compromise. It was a great victory for Rayburn whose reputation for doggedness and for legislative mastery was vastly enhanced by this exhaustive battle (039, 133).

The following year was to bring still another major legislative accomplishment for Rayburn, the Rural Electrification Act, which was to be the legislation of which he was most proud and which was also politically very appealing to his constituents (136). Congressman Marvin Jones was a close friend of Rayburn and was the chairman of the Agriculture Committee. While his committee could have exercised jurisdiction over the act, Jones claimed he gave the bill to Rayburn's Interstate and Foreign Commerce Committee since Rayburn needed a bill which would appeal to voters after the controversial and potentially politically damaging legislation with which he had been involved (052). Robert Caro claims that when Rayburn became aware of the administration's proposal, he simply demanded that the Parliamentarian of the House refer it to him and to his committee (017). Whatever the real reason for the bill's referral to Rayburn's committee, it was a tremendous political blessing for him. His rural district could vastly benefit from electrical power and rural electrification was the fastest and cheapest way of getting that power (014). For the rest of Rayburn's life, he reminded constituents of his role in passing rural electrification legislation (136). No doubt Rayburn also identified with the farmers in his district; his background was agricultural and he saw the legislation as a way of improving the lot of his people. Frequently, he talked of the burdens of farm life prior to electricity, and he seemed to have a genuine desire to bring improvements to the lives of small farmers (140).

Rural electrification was not without its enemies. The utility companies were threatened by public involvement in the power business (014, 128). Rayburn had already made enemies out of the utilities in the previous year and so he had little to lose from angering that quarter. Additionally, the utility companies had been badly discredited by the Black investigation, and so their political power was lessened during the debate over rural electrification legislation. The result was that the bill passed (039).

Thus ended the six great landmark laws of the Interstate and Foreign Commerce Committee during Rayburn´s tenure as committee chairman. It was a record of accomplishment that would be an impressive record for any Congressman. As it turned out, Rayburn, with nearly a quarter of a century of Congressional service, was still in the first half of his Congressional career. By 1936, he was regarded as a key Congressional New Dealer. He had proven that not only was he a Roosevelt loyalist, but also that he could get legislation passed. Roosevelt showed his appreciation by stopping in Denison, Texas, which was in Rayburn´s district, and announcing his approval of funds to begin a survey for the Denison Dam (039). The dam produced Lake Texoma, one of the nation´s largest man-made lakes. It was a flood control and a recreational lake, while the dam itself was a source of hydroelectric power. Development of the lake and dam created some problems, among them hostility from Oklahoma´s governor who claimed that valuable Oklahoma land would be flooded. It was also alleged that electric companies feared the public power aspects of the Denison Dam and that they prevailed upon the governor of Oklahoma to try to stop it. In spite of much noise and show, Governor Leon Phillips discovered that he could not stop the dam (075, 122, 136).

Landowners who were constituents of Rayburn were forced to sell their land for construction of the dam and the lake (144). The potential problem of unhappy constituents was partly resolved by the appointment of close Rayburn associates as appraisers and as attorneys for the government. Lee Simmons, a long time political ally of Rayburn, was appointed to assess the property of the landowners. Simmons was well known in Grayson County and Rayburn held him in great esteem. He was probably appointed to insure that landowners got a price for their land that would reduce hostility over its forced sale. Simmons could also inform Rayburn about political problems developing with specific landowners (136, 138). Fenner Leslie, another longtime Rayburn friend, was appointed special assistant to the U.S. attorney in the Land Division of the Attorney General´s Office. He worked on land acquisitions and, as he described his job:

> Sam Rayburn was solely responsible for my being appointed assistant United States attorney. I was in his district, and there was talk that he would lose votes if he took land away from the people and I tried to treat them all right. He carried Grayson [County] as well as he did Fannin County and

he didn't lose any votes in Grayson County
for that purpose (146).

Lake Texoma was the largest government project in
the district during Rayburn's Congressional career. It
covers 89,000 surface acres and can hold 2,722,000
acre-feet of water. He worked as well to bring
numerous other projects to the district. Those projects
included a major 1,500 bed veterans hospital in
McKinney, Texas; a veterans domiciliary in Bonham; air
bases in Sherman, Bonham, Greenville, and Terrell;
prisoner of war camps in Kaufman and near Farmersville;
Lake Lavon; Lake Bonham; and Lake Davy Crockett (136).
Rayburn was not always successful in his efforts to
attract government projects to the district. He, for
example, failed to get the government to locate the Air
Force Academy near Sherman (056). However, there were
enough major projects located in the district during
Rayburn's career to make his constituency aware that he
had influence over the Congressional pork barrel.

By the time Sam Rayburn was elected Speaker, he had
served in Congress for twenty seven years; yet he was
only fifty eight years old. He had served as Majority
Leader under Speaker William Bankhead for three years
and had served for six years as an extraordinarily
effective committee chairman. The Speakership offered
new challenges. He was no longer John Nance Garner's
lieutenant; he had come into his own. In fact, his
friendship with Garner had created tensions between him
and Franklin Roosevelt. Garner's relationship with
Roosevelt soured after Roosevelt proposed the Court
Packing Plan of 1937. Under the plan, one justice
would be appointed to the Court for every justice over
the age of 70 who did not retire. Assuming no
retirements, that meant that Roosevelt would be able to
appoint six new justices and would increase the size of
the Court to fifteen members. The plan was clearly in
response to Roosevelt's frustration with the Court's
unwillingness to allow him the Constitutional leeway
that he felt he needed in order to deal with the
nation's economic problems. The plan was one Roosevelt
policy which led to a major rebellion within the
Democratic Party (126). It was, as Rayburn believed, a
serious mistake (028).

Garner was so openly hostile to the plan that his
loyalty was thereafter considered questionable by
Roosevelt. Additionally, Garner became convinced that
Roosevelt would run for a third term, and Garner was a
strong believer in the two term tradition. Not only
did he refuse to support a third term; but also he
moved into the forefront of efforts to head off a third

term by running for President. He had already
concluded that the New Deal had moved into an
unacceptably leftward direction, and so he seemed quite
willing to break with Roosevelt (123). The break and
subsequent candidacy for the Presidency placed Rayburn
in a dilemma. How could he be loyal to both Garner and
to Roosevelt?

While Garner declared his candidacy for the
Presidency; Roosevelt did not. In order to overcome
the two term tradition, he needed to respond to a
draft, to be asked to serve another term instead of
declaring for the third term. As a result, he was not
a declared candidate until the 1940 Democratic
convention (125).

Rayburn was able to endorse Garner and claim that he
remained loyal to Roosevelt on the ground that
Roosevelt was not a declared candidate. Texas was
split between the pro-Roosevelt forces and the
anti-Roosevelt Garner forces, however, and so there was
an appearance of hostility to Roosevelt in Rayburn's
action (017). Even Roosevelt apparently began to doubt
the loyalty of his old ally. In honor of Rayburn, the
town of Denison sponsored a "Sam Rayburn Day" and
Rayburn's friend, Cecil Dickson, wrote Roosevelt and
asked that the President send greetings for the
occasion. Stephen Early, Roosevelt's secretary,
reminded Roosevelt of the endorsement of Garner, and
Roosevelt chose to refuse to send greetings. Instead,
he lied to Dickson and claimed that Dickson's request
did not arrive in time for the greetings to be sent
(110).

Rayburn was developing a compromise between the
pro-Roosevelt and the pro-Garner forces. He did not
want his old friend Garner to be embarrassed by losing
the support of the Texas delegation at the convention,
but he did not want the New Deal hurt by the political
turmoil in Texas either. The solution was that the
Texas delegation would endorse the New Deal, not
participate in any "Stop Roosevelt" movement, and
support Garner as a "favorite son". The compromise
created heat on both sides, but ultimately it did
protect the administration, provide Roosevelt some
Texas votes in possible later balloting if several
convention ballots proved necessary and "favorite sons"
were eliminated, and also avoided embarrassment to the
Vice-President. Robert Caro has claimed that Lyndon
Johnson attempted to take advantage of Rayburn's
tenuous position between Roosevelt and Garner by
spreading the belief that Rayburn was anti-Roosevelt.
He claimed that Johnson felt he could become the key

representative of the New Deal in Texas if Rayburn could be discredited as a New Dealer (017). Strong evidence that Johnson conspired against Rayburn is lacking, but it is clear that Roosevelt had some doubts about Rayburn during this time period and that Johnson was his instrument for expressing his displeasure. When, for example, the compromise was announced, it was at Roosevelt's insistence announced jointly by Rayburn and by Johnson. It appeared to be an effort by Roosevelt to embarrass Rayburn by making Johnson look like a co-leader of Texas Democrats. Harold Ickes, a person who was unfriendly to Rayburn, wrote that Rayburn did not want it to appear that a "kid congressman like Johnson was apparently on the same footing as himself, the majority leader" (117, pp. 167-168). However, Johnson was widely known as an extreme pro-Roosevelt Congressman and had been elected as such in a widely publicized special election. It may be that the insult to Rayburn was really an effort to showcase a promising, able, and strongly pro-Roosevelt Congressman.

It has been claimed that Johnson and Rayburn barely spoke for a year and one half after the battles over the Texas compromise (039). Within a few years, however, they developed a strong mentor-protege relationship. This time Rayburn was in a different position. In the past, he had been the protege of senior men like Joe Bailey and John Nance Garner. This time, he was the senior man mentoring a promising young politician (040).

Once Roosevelt manufactured his draft for a third term at the 1940 convention, it was time to pick another vice-presidential nominee. Garner, off the ticket, retired to his hometown of Uvalde, Texas. Rayburn had some hopes for the vice-presidential nomination. Given his leadership in the utility holding company battle, his supporters argued that he would be a logical counterpoint to Roosevelt's opponent, Wendell Wilkie, a utility holding company executive. Additionally, Rayburn's nomination might be a conciliatory move toward the Garner forces within the Democratic Party. Texas, however, had been very troublesome for Roosevelt, and it did not seem likely that the conservatives in the Democratic Party would be appeased by Rayburn's nomination. Further, another influential Texan, Jesse Jones, was a candidate for the vice-presidency. The two candidacies split Texas and lessened Rayburn's chances (131). Numerous other Democrats were candidates for the vice-presidency as well, including Speaker William Bankhead. When Roosevelt called to ask Rayburn to second the nomination of Henry Wallace for the vice-presidency, Rayburn thought he was going to be asked to be the Democratic vice-presidential nominee (079). Roosevelt, it was claimed, chose Wallace because he was strongly anti-fascist and because he had appeal in the farm belt (125). Rayburn did loyally second Wallace's nomination, although several commentators felt that there was notable reluctance to do so which was expressed in this part of Rayburn's seconding speech:

> I come to second the nomination of another. Let me say that if I consulted my loyalty to friendship and my love, I would probably be seconding the nomination of another, but under the circumstances I can do none other than follow what I believe to be the wish of our great leader (003, 125, 201).

It has frequently been claimed that Rayburn's life was the House of Representatives and that he had no higher ambition than to be Speaker of the House of Representatives (055). However, on at least five occasions, it seems clear that Rayburn's ambitions went beyond the House. In 1922, while he was still a young Congressman, he wrote his sister, Katy Thomas, that he had considered running for the U.S. Senate (192). When he wrote his brother-in-law, W.A. Thomas, in 1922, he noted that he had decided not to run for the Senate, and he added that it was in part because of the effect of Joe Bailey. Rayburn wrote, "The press of Texas is 95 percent anti-Bailey and every time he bobs up they are reminded that I am the last of the old crowd and I am punished." He noted that, when he was elected Chairman of the Democratic Caucus, no Texas paper outside his district commented editorially, even though it was "an honor of which the whole state should have been proud." He added, "There must be a reason," and he suggested it was his tie to Bailey. His connection with Joe Bailey, he felt, would discredit any statewide candidacy (205). By that time, Bailey was widely regarded as corrupt, and yet he maintained a presence in Texas and even ran for offices. Rayburn knew that in a hotly contested statewide race, which was far broader than Bailey's northeast Texas base, Rayburn's loyalty to Bailey would become an issue and would be used to discredit his candidacy. Thus, early in his career Rayburn was forced to limit his political ambitions to his House district. In 1940, Rayburn was interested in succeeding Garner as Vice-President, but the Jesse Jones candidacy, anti-Roosevelt feeling in Texas, and Roosevelt's personal preferences prevented him from achieving that ambition (003). Later in 1944, it became clear that Henry Wallace would be removed

from the ticket as the vice-presidential candidate.
Again, there is evidence that Rayburn was interested in
the Vice-Presidency. He participated in the effort to
get Wallace removed from the ticket (116), maintained
his availability for the vice-presidency, and
according to one close friend, attended a meeting with
national Democratic leaders where his candidacy was
discussed (105). It has been claimed that Roosevelt
did not choose Rayburn in 1944 because he felt Rayburn
lacked necessary knowledge of foreign affairs. Another
reason may have been that Roosevelt felt that he needed
Rayburn in the House. Party leaders may have felt that
Rayburn was too independent minded for the
vice-presidency (035). It may also be that the
experience with John Nance Garner prevented Roosevelt
from choosing a Garner ally and a fellow Texan. One
friend of Rayburn stated that he had been party to a
telephone conversation with Roosevelt during which FDR
rejected Rayburn's candidacy for the vice-presidency
with the comment that he had too many problems with a
previous vice-president from Texas (105). In 1944,
Roosevelt chose Harry Truman to be his
vice-presidential candidate. Truman had Rayburn's
support for the vice-presidency and, interestingly,
Truman had been one of the political leaders who had
been boosting Rayburn's vice-presidential candidacy
(025, 105). In 1952, a small boomlet developed for
Rayburn for President. Although at times he dismissed
such talk, at other times he seemed to approve the idea
and appeared to hope that enough support would be
generated to get him the Presidential nomination. His
was a dark horse candidacy, although it had the support
of numerous members of Congress and other influential
people in the Democratic Party. Essentially, the view
was that Rayburn could get the nomination if the
convention deadlocked between Estes Kefauver and
Richard Russell (039). Later, when that hope for the
Presidency had faded, Hale Boggs, Rayburn's close
Congressional friend from Louisiana, was shocked to
learn from Rayburn that he would be willing to accept
the vice-presidential nomination in 1956 (007, 008).
It is no doubt true that Rayburn loved the House and
that he felt the Speakership fulfilled his ambitions;
however, there was during the course of his political
career at least a spark of interest in political
offices other than the House of Representatives.

With the Vice-Presidency beyond his grasp, in 1940,
Rayburn was elected Speaker of the House of
Representatives upon the death of Speaker William
Bankhead. Roosevelt's election to a third term meant a
continuation of the Congressional teamwork that had
existed between Rayburn and Roosevelt since 1933. The

issues, however, were dramatically different from the issues upon which they worked in the early 1930s. Nazism and Japanese militarism were increasingly threatening to the United States. Aid to the Allies and preparation for war became a major concern. It was just such an issue that led to what may be Rayburn's most famous action as Speaker. It was in some ways an action that was out of character for Rayburn who became known as a powerful, but consensus-building and fair Speaker. In 1941, he made a ruling from the chair that many considered to be an arbitrary use of the powers of the Speakership. It was also an action which was to win praise for allowing the United States to be somewhat prepared for war when the attack on Pearl Harbor occurred. The issue dealt with extension of the draft. Draftees were expected to serve for 12 months and the administration wished to extend their service. Rayburn, convinced that extension of the draft was an important national security concern, supported the administration's proposal for extension of the draft.

Tremendous opposition developed to extension. Soldiers felt they had been betrayed into believing that their tour of duty would be only 12 months. Mothers of draftees mobilized against extension. Pacifist groups also opposed extension in the belief that it was a step toward mobilizing America for war. It began to look like the administration would be defeated. On several occasions Rayburn delayed the vote on extension to try to lobby the House for additional votes. Finally, when the vote was taken, it came to 203-202 in favor of extension. Rayburn, on the motion of extension opponent Congressman Dewey Short, allowed a recapitulation of the vote. However, he announced the vote without objection from Short prior to the recapitulation. The result was that votes, under the rules of the House, could not be changed. When Short then made a motion to reconsider, he was ruled out of order since that motion has to be made by one who voted for the measure. Numerous objections were then made by other members of Congress, but Rayburn held firm and the draft extension bill was passed. He was accused of unfairness in not allowing vote changes which would have defeated extension. Actually, he was within the established rules of procedure in acting as he did. It was just that he had exploited Dewey Short's lack of parliamentary knowledge. Within months, Pearl Harbor was attacked. The Speaker with a fast gavel was recognized as a Congressional leader whose actions in the heat of a major political battle enhanced the preparedness of the country in the early stages of World War II (025, 039, 084).

Throughout the war, he was a dedicated supporter of Roosevelt´s efforts in international affairs (025, 039, 084). He was one of the few Congressmen who was informed of the development of the atomic bomb. Fifteen months before the bomb was dropped on Hiroshima, he was informed by Secretary of War Henry Stimson, General George Marshall, and Dr. Vannevar Bush that an initial $800,000,000 was needed to support the project. Rayburn brought in other Congressional leaders and the Chairman of the Appropriations Committee for discussions about the project. He then requested the money from the Appropriations Committee and then from the full House, although secrecy required that the money be appropriated without explanation. By contemporary Congressional standards, it was an amazing feat. Both the Committee and the House approved the expenditure on the leaders´ promises that the money was needed to save American lives and to shorten the war (025, 039, 084).

RAYBURN´S HOME STYLE

As a Congressional leader and with war keeping Congress in session on virtually a year round basis, he had little opportunity to visit with his constituents and to keep his political fences mended. As a result, he faced one of his most significant political challenges in years when state senator G.C. Morris from Greenville, Texas, opposed him in the 1944 Democratic primary. Morris attacked Rayburn for being a yes-man for Roosevelt, for being in office too long, and he appealed to dissatisfaction with the war, with wartime rationing, and with Rayburn´s preoccupation with working in Washington on wartime legislation (136). Morris had been a very influential state senator who had gained considerable fame as a major opponent of Governor W. Lee O´Daniel´s transactions tax, a sales tax proposal to fund O´Daniel´s popular pensions for the elderly in Texas (064). Morris was young, an excellent public speaker, and well funded. The money probably came from right wing anti-New Deal conservatives. There is evidence that Hugh Roy Cullen, a wealthy oil man from Houston who was known for his anti-New Deal attitudes, was one major contributor to Morris´ campaign (047). Cullen, known as the "King of the Wildcatters," was a self-made millionaire. Beginning in 1928, he made a series of oil field discoveries, the greatest of which was the billion dollar pool of oil known as the Tom O´Connor field. Although Cullen gave away over $200 million of his fortune, he was opposed to a strong federal government, Franklin Roosevelt, and Rayburn (022, 136). In the

1950s, he was to become a leading contributor to
Senator Joe McCarthy (159). It is also said that the
Sun Oil group of companies or members of the Pew family
which controlled Sun, also funded opposition to Rayburn
for many years. J. Howard Pew, President of Sun from
1912-1947, had ultra-conservative views and supported
anti-New Deal efforts (022). Rayburn believed that
many of his opponents had over the years been funded by
the Sinclair oil interests (041). In 1948, Harry
Sinclair told Rayburn that he regretted that Rayburn
had had an opponent in 1944. Rayburn accused Sinclair
of providing most of the money used to oppose Rayburn
in that race. When Sinclair denied the accusation,
Rayburn told him, "Well, it´s hard for me to believe
that you didn´t know it, but if you don´t know, you
check with your man in Texas and find out how much
money he did spend in my district trying to beat me"
(040, p. 36).

Morris apparently didn´t need out-of-state money.
He was able to raise $56,000 for his race in the Dallas
area alone (039). There are several stories of
politicians in the Fourth Congressional District who
were approached by wealthy conservatives from outside
the district and offered money to run against Rayburn.
Rayburn´s primary opponent in 1954 was a very minor
one, and yet he showed ten one thousand dollar bills to
a friend of Rayburn and claimed that he had gotten the
money as campaign expense funds (136). District
political leaders such as Roland Boyd and R.C. Slagle
were also offered money to run against Rayburn,
although both of these men refused to do so (012, 152).
It appears that for years wealthy conservatives were
readily available to back those who would challenge
Texas´ major Congressional symbol of Franklin
Roosevelt´s New Deal (058).

Wartime pressures kept Rayburn away from his
district during part of Morris´ campaign.
Additionally, many younger men, who Rayburn could have
counted upon to campaign in his behalf, were at war.
The key supporters who remained at home tended to be
elderly men. It was possible to develop a number of
good arguments in Rayburn´s behalf, however. The
nation was at risk and, as Speaker, the district´s
Congressman was needed in Washington. Rayburn´s
speakership was a source of pride for his district and
an appeal was made that the constituents had to
recognize that the Speaker was needed for the war
effort. Morris was young, and so Rayburn´s supporters,
ignoring the exemption of public officials from
military service, began to ask why Morris was not in
the army. Additionally, they argued that Rayburn´s

lengthy service should not be criticized since he had proved that he was an effective Congressman. Emphasis was placed upon his efforts in behalf of rural electrification and Lake Texoma. It was also stressed that several military bases and prisoner of war camps had been located in the district and that they had brought economic benefits to the district (136).

While such arguments worked and Rayburn won the primary, it was a race that clearly worried Rayburn. He claimed that the reason he did not attend the 1944 Democratic convention was that he had such a hard race in the district that he could not afford to leave. Majority Leader John McCormack called him during this race and pleaded with him to attend the convention and to campaign among the delegates for the vice-presidency. McCormack told Rayburn that he could be the vice-presidential nominee if he would go to the convention. Rayburn told him the campaign against Morris prevented him from leaving the district (063). One writer has speculated that Rayburn already knew that he would not be the Democratic vice-presidential nominee and that the campaign in the district was an excuse to avoid the embarrassment of losing the nomination (058). While this charge may be correct, the seriousness of Morris' candidacy should not be minimized.

Rayburn was able to defeat Morris and his other Democratic primary opponents for a number of very important reasons. One was his political style while he was in the district. Although he strongly disliked campaigning (139), he appeared to be relaxed and informal and readily able to identify with his constituents. He had grown up on a small farm and had known poverty and the difficulties of farm life. It was an upbringing that he never forgot and that he never let his constituents forget. The people of the rural northeast Texas district had shared a similar upbringing, and he conveyed the impression that he was one of them. Rayburn tended to stress his upbringing in many of his speeches. He presented to his constituents an image of a lifelong farmer who was in government to try to relieve the burdens and drudgery of farm life (136, 148). As one of his friends described the Rayburn image,

> Many times I have heard him tell the story of his little country schooling and his mother and father. I think this is what gave him such great ties to his people. As a country kid myself, and going to a three teacher school, gosh, I could relate to that. So

could everybody in his district. We all felt
like he was one of us (153).

His behavior indicated that he sought identification
with his constituents (018, 032). "Sam," claimed one
of his political supporters, "was as common as an old
shoe" (152). He always seemed to have a plug of
tobacco in his cheek when he was in the district, and
he seemed to make an effort to spit in the fireplace of
his home when constituents were visiting. Although he
wore tailor-made suits in Washington and as Speaker he
had a chauffeur-driven limousine, in the district he
frequently wore khakis, an old shirt, old fashioned
shoes, and a slouchy hat. Instead of riding in the
Speaker's limousine in the district, the car was parked
in the garage of his home, and he rode in his
well-dented pickup truck or in his sister's Plymouth.
Once he got to Bonham, his East Texas accent became
more pronounced and the drawl thickened. In the
district, he cut his own wood and worked his own
cattle.   Prior to leaving Washington for the
district, he would study Dept. of Agriculture crop
reports so that he would be able to talk about crops
with the farmers of the district (018, 136).

He also maintained a simple life style which
projected an image of honesty. He was quite proud of
his reputation for honesty and for being a man of his
word. He made efforts to avoid the appearance of any
conflicts of interest. After he went to Congress, he
did not maintain a law office at home and he made it a
practice to own no stocks or bonds. His savings were
kept in a checking account, U.S. savings bonds, or were
invested in his farm or ranch. He accepted no
honorariums for speeches and frequently paid his own
expenses when he was invited to speak. His ethics were
not unnoticed, nor did they go unmentioned in his
political campaigns (018, 136). In a speech in Bonham
in 1922, for example, he said, "I have been unable to
save much money in my life. I have been in politics,
and an honest man in politics does not get rich. I
have been kept broke by making campaigns in this
district every two years. But every dollar that I have
saved has been invested in a little farm" (194). A
1932 election flyer stated, "We submit that Sam Rayburn
owns no stocks or bonds, but that his savings are in a
farm in Fannin County; that he was reared on a farm and
that, therefore he has the interests of the farmer at
heart..." (154). He took great pride in being a man of
his word and he never gave promises lightly. With the
image of unpretentiousness and personal honesty came
the image that he was a man who could be trusted by his
constituents.

The stress on personal character was an important one for Rayburn. As one of his political supporters in the district pointed out,

> He would go around and meet people around over the district. He wouldn't promise all sorts of things he knew he probably couldn't deliver on. He tried to tell them something about himself; what kind of man he was. And then, in effect, he said to them, "If you think I am the kind of man you can feel comfortable with having as your representative in Washington, then I would like your vote. Otherwise, then you should vote for somebody else. I can't sit here now and tell you how I am going to vote on all these issues that are going to come up in the next two years, but I will tell you this: I will vote on each one of them only after a study of the pros and cons and I'll vote to the best of my judgement and conscience (143).

Rayburn's success in bringing such projects to the district as rural electrification and Lake Texoma undoubtedly explains support for him from persons who were interested in the economic development of the district. Rayburn did not overlook the political implications of these projects. In Bonham, for example, he worked to locate a veterans' hospital and domiciliary. That project provided 350 government jobs to a community whose wage scale tended to be considerably less than the government pay scale. Most of these positions were civil service, but on the same day that the personnel officer for the facility moved to Bonham, Rayburn met with him and discussed the importance of hiring local people. For the next three years the personnel officer held regular meetings with Rayburn in which Rayburn informed him of constituents who were interested in positions, and the personnel officer informed Rayburn of vacancies and civil service examination times and dates. Rayburn's interests in constituents, the stuff of legends today in the Fourth Congressional District, led him to be concerned with the appointment of nurses, groundkeepers, cooks, and butchers at the domiciliary at the same time that he was serving as Speaker of the United States during the Korean conflict (145).

His great concern with constituent interests in the Veterans Hospital and Domiciliary was not unique. Once a conflict developed in Rains County over a rural mail carrier's position. Two of Rayburn's friends were

applicants. Rayburn went to Rains County to discuss
the problem with his political leader in the county and
to work out a solution (150). When the Sam Rayburn
Library hired a janitor in 1957, Rayburn considered the
political implications of hiring an unusually able
black man to the position for which he had several
white applicants. Although he ultimately decided to
hire the black man, he considered the political
implications of the hiring even though by 1957 he had
been in Congress for forty-four years, had no serious
political opposition for nine years, and was a
political institution in his district (136).

Even in Washington, his attention to constituents
was so careful and cultivating that it seems unreal in
the more impersonal political times of the 1980s. When
in Washington, he would call Bonham daily for reports
on constituents' needs and interests (136). He even
enlisted his sister, Miss Lou, to keep the personnel
officer of the domiciliary informed of constituents'
employment desires. She would receive calls from her
brother and the next day invite the personnel officer
to the Rayburn house for cake and messages from Mr. Sam
(145). He had a staff member clip items from local
newspapers such as wedding information, funerals,
births, marriages, and school honor rolls. Letters
would then be sent with an appropriate message from
Congressman Rayburn (057). If constituents visited
Washington, Rayburn insisted upon greeting them. Once
a staff member felt the brunt of Rayburn's famed temper
when he allowed a farm couple who were from the
district, but who had no special political connection
with Rayburn, to leave Rayburn's office in the Capitol
without first visiting with him. After making the
staff member search the Capitol to find the
constituents, visiting with them, and arranging for
them to have lunch with him and be driven back to their
hotel in the Speaker's limousine, he explained to the
young staff member, "These are the people I represent.
These are the people that pay my salary. These are the
most important people, more important than the guy who
is out there with the appointment wanting something.
These people are not wanting something other than good
representation" (013).

With such attention to constituents, it should not
be surprising that over the years, he was able to
develop a remarkable network of political volunteers
who campaigned in Rayburn's behalf and who got out the
vote. This district-wide network was composed of
personal friends, ambitious politicians, those seeking
patronage, those who had received or desired to

receive favors from Rayburn, and civic-minded citizens who saw Rayburn as someone who had helped and who could help their communities. They would give speeches in Rayburn's behalf, contribute small amounts of money to his campaigns, buy newspaper ads and announcements for him, urge friends and relatives to vote for Rayburn, and keep Rayburn informed of the opposition. Over time, Rayburn's network of volunteers crossed as many as three generations where sons would work in Rayburn's behalf because their fathers and grandfathers had done so. The network was a loosely knit organization which usually had at its apex one or two leaders of each county in the district. These men functioned as Rayburn's closest political advisors on district matters, and he depended upon them to maintain political support for him, especially during the time he would be in Washington. When he returned to the district, he would frequently meet with the leaders, and constituents would ask the leaders to seek aid in their behalf from Rayburn (136). Rayburn would also maintain an open door policy for constituents while he was in the district; any constituent could come to see him at his home even without an appointment, could seek assistance, or simply offer opinions to Rayburn. One of the most difficult tasks for the Rayburn staff member who was asked to return from Washington to the district with Rayburn was to fit constituents without appointments in between the schedules of constituents who came to Rayburn's house with appointments (029).

His large family aided Rayburn's first campaign. That was a pattern which continued for many years after he went to the U.S. Congress. His brother Frank, a physician who died in 1928, worked long hours in Rayburn's behalf and was well known in Fannin County. Brother Tom was younger than Sam and was a farmer in the Bonham area. As the long time superintendent of the livestock barn at the Fannin County Fair, he was frequently in contact with other farmers. He would attend Sam's political rallies and would campaign for his brother among friends and neighbors. As a young man, he had played baseball throughout northeast Texas and was so well known as a baseball player that it was said he had better name recognition in the district than did brother Sam during his earliest years in politics. That fame made Tom a considerable political asset. Brother Jim worked for years as a rural mail carrier. He would informally poll customers on his mail route to get a sense of political attitudes in the district. Dick was politically the most active of Sam's brothers. He was in the cottonseed oil business and worked with farmers all over the district. He used these trips to interact with Sam's key supporters throughout the district and to gather information for his brother. Considered the friendliest and most outgoing of the family, he had a wide circle of friends and excellent political judgement. W.A. Thomas was the husband of Katherine Rayburn, Sam's sister. He originally was from Hunt County, then lived in Fannin County, then moved to Dallas and became director of the Internal Revenue Service in Dallas. Until his death in 1946, he retained a strong interest in politics. He had been a Joe Bailey supporter. In 1928, he had played a major role in the Smith-Robinson presidential campaign and was an early supporter of Texas' long time U.S. Senator, Tom Connally. He frequently contacted friends in Rayburn's behalf and coordinated Rayburn's appearances throughout the district. He also apparently provided some help to Rayburn through contacts he had in other states in Rayburn's effort to become Majority Leader in 1936. Robert Bartley was Sam Rayburn's nephew. He was fascinated by politics, and in the late 1930s and early 1940s he became active in Rayburn's campaigns in the district, and he later worked as Administrative Assistant to Rayburn in Washington. During the Truman years, Bartley was, with Rayburn's support, appointed as a Federal Communications Commissioner. By the 1940s, however, most of the family's political activities began to be performed by nonfamily members who volunteered to work in Rayburn's behalf and who became part of his loose knit political organization (005, 030, 059, 136).

One of the politically most useful characteristics of Rayburn's district was that it was not a rapidly changing one. The changes that did occur in his district never created political dangers for Rayburn. Over his half century in politics, more people moved to the towns and fewer lived in the countryside. The farmers were less isolated. There was little in-migration, and the district actually lost population during Rayburn's Congressional tenure. When Rayburn was elected to Congress in 1912, his district had five counties--Fannin, Grayson, Rains, Hunt and Collin--and a total population of 214,721. By 1930 the district had experienced a population decline of over 5,000 people, even though the population of Texas had increased by nearly 50%. With redistricting in 1934, two counties--Kaufman and Rockwall--were added to his district, increasing its population to 257,879. By 1960, even with the additional two counties in 1934, Rayburn's district only had a population of 216,371. There were no large cities in his district and there were only five towns with a population greater than 10,000. In 1960, Sherman, the largest town in the district, had a population of only 24,988. Three of the counties in Rayburn's seven county district--Fannin, Rains, and Rockwall Counties--had no town with a population as large as 10,000. If his district had been apportioned according to the requirement of one person-one vote, it would have had to have a population of approximately 435,000 and it would have logically included part of the conservative, urban Dallas County to the south, which had a Congressional district with a population of over 950,000 (136).

Cotton was the main crop and agriculture was the main industry. Within the district, in 1960, 14.4% of those who were employed were employed in agriculture compared to 8.7% for Texas as a whole, and only 52.9% of the district's population were living in communities of more than 2,500 people compared to 75% of the population of Texas as a whole. With a family median income in 1960 that was nearly $1,000 per year less than the family median income for Texas and a median education for those over the age of 25 that was nearly one year less than the median education for Texas, the district was a small, rural, farming district with a population of poorly educated, relatively poor people compared to the remainder of the state. It was the kind of district that could elect a man who identified with small farmers, knew his neighbors, and had populist political values. As a result, Rayburn never had to contend with changing political interests within his district, with Republicans, or with increasing population. With the exception of one redistricting in 1934, when two rural counties were added to his district, Rayburn never experienced the problems associated with building new political bases in redistricted areas. In his later years, Rayburn had a district with one of the smallest populations in the United States. Not only did it remain rural, but without in-migration Rayburn was able to develop some contact with almost all of the established families in the district and was able to gain votes from them as a result of the personal relationships that he had developed with them (136). From time to time, his political enemies in Austin would threaten to redistrict Rayburn in order to upset the close and comfortable relationship he had generally established with the district, and possibly those enemies might even have been able to defeat Rayburn through redistricting (072). However, Rayburn's power was such that even many of his enemies realized that he was too useful to Texas to allow him to be redistricted out of office. Additionally, over the years he had developed a strong network of friends and supporters in Austin which would have made any redistricting attempt aimed at harming Rayburn a very difficult one (156, 179).

THE TRUMAN YEARS

With the end of the war and the election of Harry Truman, Rayburn gained a friend in the White House who shared his values and much of his background. Although Rayburn liked Roosevelt and generally worked well with him, it was Truman for whom he felt genuine friendship, and Truman shared that feeling for Rayburn. After Truman left the White House, it was his old friend Rayburn to whom he turned for aid in getting a pension in order that he might live in retirement without accepting positions which might have created ethical problems for Truman and which in Truman's mind would have demeaned the Presidency (039). President Truman claimed that he frequently relied on Rayburn for counsel and that Rayburn's advice was often a moderating force (132). Rayburn apparently felt that Truman could sometimes be impetuous in his decision making and Rayburn saw himself as a steadying force in the Truman Administration (152).

In spite of the great personal affection between the two men, they were not always in agreement. Civil rights, in particular, was the issue area that probably represented the greatest gulf between them. Truman was a strong advocate for civil rights. He supported the integration of the armed forces, the creation of a civil rights commission, federal legislation against lynching, a ban on the poll tax, and a fair employment practices act. Rayburn represented a rural Texas district which still maintained strong memories of the Civil War and the Confederacy and which had deeply held Southern values. It was politically impossible for him to support civil rights legislation (136).

Rayburn avoided public criticism of Truman's civil rights proposals except in his district where another primary battle in 1948 against G.C. Morris caused him to declare his opposition to the proposals (203). Morris capitalized on opposition to Truman and civil rights by claiming that Rayburn was supporting civil rights. Once Rayburn publicly declared his opposition, Morris' main issue against Rayburn was vastly weakened (136). In his earlier years, Rayburn held traditional Southern racial views and gave strong segregationist speeches. In 1922, for example, he said, "Some have gone to the negroes and paid their poll taxes to get them to vote for them. I do not make this as a threat, but the negroes of Fannin County are not going to vote in this coming primary. By the Eternal God, my ancestor´s blood has been spilled on nearly every hill on this land, that this should be a white man´s country" (195). It had been many years since he had made such speeches. As a leader of the national Democratic Party, it was politically inappropriate for him to do so. However, some observers have argued that over the years, Rayburn had modified his racial views and that he had genuinely favorable views about blacks in his later years (058, 136). On one occasion he was faced with an incident that illustrated how Rayburn handled racial issues in those later years. During the 1950s, he received a request for an appointment in Washington, D.C., with a visiting delegation of school-children from the district. A staff member pointed out that the children were black and asked Rayburn if he would see them. Rayburn, who took great pleasure in visiting with school-children, unhesitatingly agreed to the appointment. When the time came for the visit, Rayburn arranged to lunch with the children in his office and supplied soft drinks, sandwiches and potato chips. He treated the children well and won their friendship. However, this display of friendliness toward blacks was not made in public, nor were any reporters told of the visit. It was contrary to his usual practice to lunch in his office, he would usually eat in a far more visible dining area (034).

Politically, his support was necessary for the passage of the civil rights bill by the House in 1956 and for the passage of the Civil Rights Act by the Congress in 1957 (009, 010). As he told Congressman Carl Albert, it was important to pass that legislation because it was not only good for the party, but blacks had waited long enough for the legislation (002). He disliked the school desegregation decision, <u>Brown v. Board of Education</u>, in 1954, but he counseled compliance with it (209). While he may have retained segregationist views, by the mid-1950s he did not believe blacks should be denied the right to vote, and in the late 1940s he expressed personal dislike for the poll tax (136). Thus, his position in the party and his own views probably combined to make his stated opposition to Truman´s program one that was limited to speeches within the district and one in which the opposition was stated in restrained language (039, 058, 136). The Morris challenge, however, did force him to state, "No one in Congress thinks that Congress has the power to destroy the segregation laws of the state or if it did that it would be silly enough to try. If it should be attempted, I shall do all in my power to prevent it and I believe that I can prevent such an act in my present position" (203).

With his opposition to Truman's proposals, his hand was strengthened in his battle with Morris. Additionally, younger supporters who had been in the war in 1944 were home, and they organized a strong campaign in Rayburn's behalf. The result was that in 1948 Rayburn won a resounding victory against Morris. Although he was to be challenged by other opponents in 1952 and 1954, Rayburn never again faced a serious primary threat (136, 139). Interestingly, Rayburn seems to have initially thought Truman would be defeated in 1948 (085, 152). He changed his mind after he saw Truman in action during the whistle stop campaigns and after he saw the crowd's responses to Truman's speeches (152). During the Truman campaign, Bonham was a major stop on the campaign tour of Texas (112). It was a major stop at the request of Rayburn (112), and Truman drew a gigantic crowd there. After the speech, Rayburn held a reception for Truman and thousands attended. Rayburn evidenced his close ties to his constituents when he proceeded to personally name most of the guests in introducing them to President Truman (025, 084, 136).

Although Rayburn was unable to support Truman's civil rights proposals, generally his district gave him great leeway in making decisions as to which legislation he would support or oppose. The Taft-Hartley Act, for example, was popular in his district which, with the exception of Denison's railroad unions, had little organized labor and which tended to be hostile to union activities. Nevertheless, as Speaker he took the administration's position and opposed the act which was restrictive of labor unions. Rayburn had not been known for his prolabor stance since 1940 and had done little to block antilabor legislation. However, he publicly opposed the Hartley bill even though he knew it would pass. Rayburn spoke to the House, argued the bill was an unfair one, and voted against it. Not even the Texas delegation stood by him on the measure, and it passed the House by a vote of 308-107 (039, 136). Lyndon Johnson, closest protege of Mr. Sam, voted against the Hartley Bill since he was running for the U.S. Senate from Texas and felt that he needed to prove his conservatism (027). When the legislation was vetoed by President Truman, Rayburn, along with only two other Texas Congressmen, voted to sustain the veto (039).

THE EISENHOWER YEARS

The election of Dwight Eisenhower in 1952 dramatically changed Rayburn's role. Eisenhower's victory brought with it a Republican controlled House of Representatives. Thus Rayburn, who had been Speaker since 1940 except for two years when the Democrats were in the minority in 1947-1948, was now in the minority. He apparently considered retiring from the leadership when that occurred, not feeling comfortable as minority leader after having served as Speaker for so long (010). The structure of the House of Representatives is such that the majority usually can control the policy making process. Members of the minority party have far less influence upon policy making and frequently can do little else than oppose the policy initiatives of the majority. With a Republican president and a Republican majority in the senate, the weakness of a minority Congressman is enhanced even further (051). Twice before he had considered retirement from the House of Representatives. When the Republicans gained control of the House in 1947, he had briefly considered leaving the House or at least leaving the Democratic leadership (039). He again considered it when he thought Harry Truman would be defeated. He had talked to one close friend about wanting to retire and to farm (085). Truman's success as a candidate apparently dissuaded Rayburn once he concluded that Truman would be the victor in the presidential race. Later he told a friend that he would not have retired in those years unless he thought Republicans would remain the dominant party (039).

In 1952, he talked more in terms of remaining in Congress as a kind of elder statesman of the House. The problem was that he had no successor who appealed to the diverse factions of the Democratic Party as he did. John McCormack, the long time Democratic majority leader, did not have either the appeal of Sam Rayburn or the support Rayburn had. It seemed clear that Rayburn's absence from the leadership would bring with it a hard fight for the Democratic leader's position. Finally, at the urging of a number of Democrats, including McCormack, Rayburn stepped down from the Speakership and became the Democratic minority leader (009, 010, 207). Joe Martin of Massachusetts, the Republican leader and a close friend of Rayburn, became the Speaker (060).

Dwight Eisenhower and Rayburn got along well on a personal level, although Rayburn felt that Eisenhower lacked political leadership qualities and that he did not work as conscientiously as he should (091). Members of Eisenhower's administration sometimes were so partisan in their views that they distrusted Rayburn, the old Democratic partisan. Rayburn genuinely believed in a bipartisan foreign policy and yet was frustrated by the administration in his desire to achieve bipartisanship (040). Rayburn promised Eisenhower that he would have his support if Ike wished to extend existing Democratic programs. Attempts to reverse policies on public power, reclamation, public housing, taxes, and farm assistance would likely be opposed by Rayburn. Because the GOP was badly split and because it only had a one vote majority in the Senate and a ten vote majority in the House, Eisenhower needed Rayburn's support. In 1953, when Rayburn was in the minority, he supported Eisenhower on 74% of the issues that <u>Congressional Quarterly</u> classified as Eisenhower-issue roll call votes. <u>Congressional Quarterly</u> ranked Rayburn ninth among Democrats in the House of Representatives in support for Ike (039). Yet, Eisenhower and Rayburn split badly during Ike's first administration on some proposals such as a $20 per person tax cut. Ike concluded that the proposal was an election measure by the Democrats which was designed to cast the President and his party in a negative light and he felt insulted by Rayburn who strongly supported the cut (162). On another measure, Johnson and Rayburn supported a bill to exempt independent gas producers from federal price regulation. Although Truman had vetoed such a bill, Eisenhower was viewed as more sympathetic to deregulation. The legislation passed the House by only six votes, and Rayburn was only able to achieve that victory because he scheduled the vote when he knew the northern, urban Democrats who opposed the bill would be out of town. Although the bill passed the Senate, Eisenhower vetoed the measure amid charges that a gas lobbyist had tried to bribe Senator Francis Case by offering him a large campaign contribution (039, 165, 166). One close Congressional ally of Rayburn claimed that he was in Rayburn's hideaway room in the basement of the Capitol when Eisenhower called and told Rayburn that he was going to veto the bill. Rayburn said, "Mr. President, that is no reason. That is just a damned excuse," and he hung up the telephone (175).

Attacks from leading Republicans upon Roosevelt, Truman, and the Democratic Party angered Rayburn. Richard Nixon's bitter attacks upon the Democratic Party pained Rayburn particularly, and he came to dislike and to distrust Nixon. He told friends that Richard Nixon was a dishonest man, and he tried to minimize all personal contact with Nixon, although he did treat him with civility when it was required by protocol (091).

The Eisenhower candidacy for the presidency in 1952 had enormous impact upon Rayburn's role in Texas politics as well. The Texas Republican Party traditionally was small with primarily patronage oriented interests. By the early 1950s, it was interested increasingly in being a conservative counterpoint to what it perceived as a liberal state Democratic Party. The fight for the 1952 Republican nomination caused the orientation of the Republican Party in Texas to change from an ultra-conservative club primarily interested in patronage to a conservative broadly based organization with hopes for power within Texas. The old guard in the Republican Party supported Taft for the nomination, and the Eisenhower victory at the Republican convention allowed the forces of change to enter the Texas Republican Party (070).

Within the Democratic Party as well, Eisenhower's candidacy brought change. A strong pro-Eisenhower movement developed within the party, a movement whose close counterpart was the Hoovercrat movement of 1928. It was led by Democratic Governor Allan Shivers who claimed he supported Eisenhower because the Democratic candidate, Adlai Stevenson, held anti-Texas views on the tidelands issue (069, 157, 161, 172, 177, 185). That issue involved ownership of the rights to oil off the Texas coast. Oil had been discovered off the coasts of California, Texas, and Louisiana in the late 1930s and the states began leasing the submerged lands to oil producers. There were doubts about the states' ownership of the lands and in 1945, a test case was filed against the state of California by the U.S. government. Although Congress passed quit-claim legislation, Truman vetoed the bill. Finally, in 1947, the Supreme Court ruled against California and held that the national government had claim to the tidelands. Texas claimed that the California decision was not applicable to its tidelands since it had not ceded them to the United States when it became part of the Union. Instead, claimed Texas, its claim to submerged lands extended for three leagues, slightly over 10 miles (177).

Rayburn privately had doubts about Texas' claim; although he pushed through the House quit-claim legislation in the state's behalf. Because the measure failed in the Senate, pressure from Texas continued to build on the Speaker, and so he proposed a compromise which apparently had the endorsement of President Truman and Attorney General Tom Clark. Under the compromise, Texas, California, and Louisiana would have the rights to two-thirds of the oil and gas within three leagues and one third from there to the continental shelf which was approximately 125 miles

offshore. Rayburn had consulted with geologists who
assured him that there were vast quantities of oil
between 10 and 125 miles offshore and so Rayburn felt
the compromise would be very beneficial to Texas.
Texas Attorney General Price Daniel rejected the
compromise because, according to Rayburn, he wanted an
issue upon which to run for higher office. Daniel's
decision forced Shivers, who had initially favored the
compromise, to change his mind and oppose it. The
rejection of the compromise eventually led to a 1950
Supreme Court decision in which the national government
was held to be owner of all submerged lands off Texas'
shores. With the Supreme Court decision, Rayburn again
worked in the House to pass quit-claim legislation
while Lyndon Johnson made similar efforts in the
Senate. When the quit-claim legislation passed
Congress in 1952, it was vetoed by President Truman and
the veto could not be overridden. With the failure of
Texas' claim, Truman became the enemy, and the
statewide reaction was such that it was easy to use the
national administration as a whipping boy. Such state
leaders as Shivers and Daniel were intensely
conservative and were unfriendly to many of the
policies of the New Deal and the Fair Deal. The
tidelands issue provided the major justification for
their break with the Democratic Party's candidate for
President (039, 073, 161, 179).

Many in the Texas Democratic Party were convinced
that Shivers had no intention of supporting the
Democratic nominee in 1952, and the loyalists within
the Democratic Party sent a delegation opposing the
Shivers delegation to the national convention (164,
181). Rayburn was a loyalist and he was chairman of
the convention. He met with Shivers and later claimed
that Shivers promised him that he would support the
Democratic nominee. Shivers claimed that no such
promise was made; instead he said that he "had no
intention of not supporting the nominee...." It was,
argued Shivers, a post-convention meeting during which
Adlai Stevenson expressed support for the Truman
position on the tidelands that led him to support
Eisenhower (179, 180). Whatever did happen, Rayburn
supported the seating of the Shivers delegation.

Shortly after Stevenson received the Democratic
nomination, Shivers had sought a meeting with him and
questioned Stevenson about his attitudes toward the
tidelands. Stevenson shared the views of the Truman
Administration: He felt that the national government
owned the tidelands. Eisenhower's views on the
tidelands, on the other hand, were much more compatible
with the views of the state's leadership. He promised

to support quit-claim legislation over all of the national government´s claims to the tidelands. Claiming that he was responding to Stevenson´s hostility to Texas´ claim, Shivers, along with other state officials, endorsed Eisenhower and ran for office in 1952 on both the Democratic and Republican tickets (179, 180).

Rayburn, as a long time Democratic Party leader, felt betrayed by Shivers and was outraged by the support given to Eisenhower by Democratic officials. As a life-long Democrat, he had strong personal feelings of party loyalty, such as he had evidenced in his support of Al Smith in 1928. Additionally, as a leader of the Democratic Party in the House of Representatives, his role compelled him to vehemently oppose party disloyalty (136). Rayburn became the manager of the 1952 Stevenson campaign in Texas. It was poorly organized and poorly funded (040) since much of the campaign money usually donated by Texas oil men and relied upon by Democratic politicians was contributed instead to Eisenhower´s campaign. Only a few of the wealthiest oil men who were involved in campaign finance, men like J.R. Parten and James Abercrombie, remained dependable sources of campaign funds for Democratic loyalists (035).

It was not only oil men and state officials who abandoned the Democratic Party in 1952; many Democratic members of Congress from Texas supported Eisenhower or were noticeably uninvolved in the Stevenson campaign. Simply stated, it was politically risky in Texas to be a Stevenson Democrat. Lyndon Johnson, for example, had been elected to the U.S. Senate in 1948. In his early years in the House of Representatives, he had been a dedicated New Dealer. Enthusiasm for the New Deal waned in Texas, however, and Johnson became increasingly conservative. Identified as a strong New Dealer in 1941, he had been defeated in a special senate election by the ultra-conservative Governor of Texas, W. Lee O´Daniel. When he ran for the Senate in 1948 against another ultra-conservative, Governor Coke Stevenson, he tried to identify Stevenson as more liberal than he. He also was a critic of the Truman Administration. Having won his Senate seat by only 87 votes and having the legitimacy of those votes questioned, Johnson lacked political security. Shivers in 1952 was very popular in Texas, and Johnson was fearful that Shivers would run for the Senate against Johnson and that Shivers could defeat him. Under the circumstances, it is not surprising that Johnson tried to curry Shivers´ favor. Johnson frequently called Shivers to seek his advice and was concerned that his activities within the Democratic Party would provoke Shivers (027).

At the same time, whatever tensions there may have been between Rayburn and Johnson in the Roosevelt-Garner dispute of 1940 had long disappeared. Johnson had carefully cultivated his relationship with Rayburn. He frequently visited with Rayburn, drank with him at the Board of Education meetings, had him to dinner with the Johnson family on weekends, and acted toward Rayburn with great deference and respect. Rayburn had been virtually adopted as a member of the Johnson family, and he thought of Johnson as a son. Johnson's family--Ladybird and the girls--were like the family that Rayburn never had (017). Given his precarious political position in 1952, however, Johnson asked for Shivers' permission before he agreed to Rayburn's request to introduce Stevenson at a Ft. Worth rally (027).

No bitterness seems to have resulted from Johnson's nervousness over supporting Stevenson. Rayburn was a politician, and he understood the necessities of politics. Johnson had to protect himself from a Shivers attack until he was sure he had sufficient strength in Texas to withstand the attack. By cautiously supporting Stevenson, Johnson placated Shivers. That support maintained the respectability of Johnson's Democratic credentials for involvement in party matters in later years.

It was not long until Johnson would get increasingly involved in Democratic Party matters. With the 1952 elections, the Democratic leader in the U.S. Senate, Ernest McFarland, was defeated and the Democrats were the minority party in the Senate. Johnson ran for the Democratic leadership position and won. The result was that Texas was represented by the leaders of the Democratic Party in both the House and Senate (031). It was to prove a superb working relationship between the old Democratic partisan in the House and the young, aggressive and ambitious Johnson in the Senate. There were very different men at different stages in their lives. Rayburn was short, thick bodied, powerfully built, with a completely bald head and a granite like visage. Although he had a temper that when aroused led him to curse and to literally turn purple with rage, he was usually calm, quiet, and seemingly relaxed (017). He disliked many modern conveniences and preferred to minimize some of the prerequisites of his office such as flights in military planes or large staffs. His office had only one phone line; he preferred flying tourist class when he had to fly, although he vastly

preferred train travel (040). He had a sense of
dedication to his constituents, and he wanted to be
accessible to them. His small staff was designed to
serve the needs of his constituents, and he received
little staff assistance in dealing with
non-constituent related issues. Pretense was unknown
to Rayburn. He was comfortable talking with persons of
all social classes. He was usually affable and yet
very quiet (136). Within the Congress, he had a sense
of perspective that younger men lacked. He had known
thousands of Congressmen and had come to judge people
by their character. Rayburn admired honesty and
integrity; for him wealth was unimportant. He had seen
issues and legislation make appearances on the
legislative agenda for nearly 40 years, and he had
developed the attitude that an issue lost one year
might be won the next. He also recognized that many of
the problems that appeared to be pressing ones were not
so at all, and that they would resolve themselves if
left alone (017, 040).

Johnson was tall and had sharp features. Until the
1950s he was quite thin; then he began gaining weight
and became heavy set. Johnson was ruthless and
extremely self-serving in his behavior. Not only did
he enjoy power, but also he sought wealth and gained
great wealth in the communications business. His
television station was the only station in the Austin,
Texas, broadcasting area, a characteristic frequently
explained by noting that Johnson had great influence as
a U.S. senator. Johnson did not appear dedicated to
maintaining a life of integrity, nor did he conduct
himself with dignity. He was notoriously unfaithful to
his wife and was frequently coarse and vulgar. Like
Rayburn he had a hot temper; unlike Rayburn he was
frequently rude to people and extremely demanding. He
was legendary in the way he demanded work from his
staff. Johnson liked large staffs; he liked
technology. He was addicted to the use of the
telephone, and he had great difficulty sitting still or
relaxing. He saw politics in terms of innumerable
issues demanding urgent action (017). Johnson greatly
enjoyed the prerequisites of office, once ordering two
air force jets to fly Rayburn and himself, although
Rayburn preferred a tourist class ticket on Braniff
(040).

It is difficult to imagine that such a close bond
could exist between such different men. Yet, Johnson
was very deferential toward Rayburn and described
Rayburn as being "just like a daddy to me". Johnson
described his other mentors in this fashion, men like
Alvin Wirtz and Richard Russell, but these were men

with whom Johnson had a close relationship and who
served a mentor role for Johnson. In the last few
years of Rayburn´s life, he seemed to establish a
personal goal of promoting Lyndon Johnson for the
Presidency (017). To friends who were amazed at the
affection and regard that Rayburn held for Johnson,
Rayburn simply stated, "Lyndon´s good for Texas" (023).

Once Johnson was elected Democratic leader in the
Senate, the two were a particularly formidable pair.
Of the two men, Rayburn was clearly the best liked and
the most trusted (048, 076, 087). Rayburn disliked
Congressmen mentioning Johnson´s flaws and would
discipline Congressmen who criticized Johnson. For
example, Congressman Frank Thompson of New Jersey,
criticized Johnson in a speech which he delivered in
his home state. Rayburn called Thompson into his
office, admonished him not to criticize the Democratic
leader of the Senate, and then asked him to resign his
position as a Congressional member of the board of what
is now Kennedy Stadium in Washington, D.C. (087).
Because Johnson did not have the secure political base
that Rayburn had and because Texas as a whole was
conservative politically, Johnson tended to be
conservative. Johnson the Texas senator was to the
right of Johnson the New Deal Congressman from Austin,
Texas. Because of his state-wide presence and his
conservatism, Johnson had a closer relationship to the
right wing of the Texas Democratic Party than Rayburn
did. He cultivated Governor Shivers, had many
political friends who had backed Eisenhower in 1952,
and in addition to his close ties to the Brown & Root
company, he had financial support from many
conservative and very wealthy Texas oil men (017, 027).
Rayburn had friends in the oil business, but felt
abandoned by many of them in 1952 (040). Both men
steadfastly protected oil interests in Washington, and
it was their efforts which probably protected the oil
depletion allowance for so many years. That allowance
let oil men deduct 27.5% of their income from their
taxes before they paid taxes. The influence of oil on
state politics in those days was considerable; Johnson
and Rayburn promoted Texas interests by promoting oil
interests, obtained campaign funds, and built a
reservoir of political support within the Texas
political system (136).

Eisenhower´s first term saw Rayburn and Johnson
working closely together as Congressional leaders and
protecting Texas interests. In general, their approach
to Congressional leadership was to adopt a cooperative
approach toward working with the Eisenhower
Administration. Liberals in the Democratic Party were

quite critical of that approach, arguing that the Democratic Party should force issues such as civil rights and should move the country in a progressive direction rather than support the staid conservatism of Eisenhower. Rayburn and Johnson argued that Eisenhower was highly popular and that confrontation with the Eisenhower Administration would damage the Democratic Party. While liberals suspected that Rayburn and Johnson cooperated with the Eisenhower Administration more out of support for its conservatism than out of a desire to maintain the strength of the Democratic Party, they were unable to force Johnson or Rayburn to redirect their behavior. All they could do was to develop a voice in both the House and Senate to provide a counterweight to existing conservative voices (039).

In the House of Representatives, liberals formed an organization which became known as the Democratic Study Group. It was to be the focal point for liberal proposals and coalition building in the House. Some members of Congress felt that Rayburn perceived that group as threatening but that he infiltrated the Group with enough friends to insure that the Group would not endanger his position in the House (080). Additionally, some feel that he was sometimes able to use the Democratic Study Group as a bargaining chip in his negotiations with the conservative wing of the Democratic Party in the House. He would go to conservatives and assert that they should support a measure because a more liberal measure might be passed by the liberals if the conservatives were uncompromising (015). The opposite argument would be made with the liberals, that they had to compromise or the conservatives would kill proposed legislation (015, 080).

Allan Shivers claimed that he ran for reelection as Governor in 1954 in reaction to Rayburn´s boast that he would see to it that Shivers never held office again (179). While Shivers was successful in that 1954 campaign for the governorship, the last Shivers administration lacked the high level of support in Texas that Shivers had in earlier years. Scandal had damaged the prestige of his administration. Nevertheless, he sought to lead the Texas delegation to the 1956 Democratic convention. It was clearly a conservative delegation that would be led, and there was no doubt that Shivers was planning to repeat the 1952 campaign by remaining a Democrat, leading the delegation to the Democratic convention, and then supporting Eisenhower for the Presidency. Shivers made several very crucial miscalculations. He was then a

retiring governor, and a governor hurt by scandal.
Additionally, Johnson was then politically secure,
having won reelection in 1954 with overwhelming
strength. Finally, Rayburn was completely dedicated to
the idea that Shivers would not be allowed a repeat
performance of his behavior in the 1952 Presidential
election (039, 179).

Rayburn had to force Johnson's hand in order to
achieve his objective. Johnson tended to be remarkably
indecisive when faced with decisions affecting his
political future (081), and Johnson could not decide to
challenge Shivers for leadership of the Texas
delegation. Rayburn, without a statewide position and
with a reputation as a New Dealer, was politically
weaker in Texas than Johnson was and would have been a
poor choice to head the delegation. Additionally,
Rayburn was to be chairman of the Democratic convention
as he had been in 1948 and in 1952. Rayburn granted an
interview with a reporter from his home town paper, the
Bonham Daily Favorite, and in the interview he proposed
Johnson as a favorite son candidate to head the Texas
delegation to the convention. With his candidacy
thrust before the public by Rayburn, Johnson acquiesced
in challenging Shivers for leadership of the
delegation. It was a hard fought battle in which a
victorious coalition was built between old line
Democratic loyalists, strong Democratic liberals, and
old Shivercrats who wished to return to the party
since the tidelands issue had been settled and since
Shivers' leadership was perhaps waning (039). Johnson
headed the delegation but discovered that the liberal
wing of the party was uncooperative. Given the
strength of the conservative wing of the Democratic
Party in Texas, an effort to reintroduce them into the
party no doubt appeared politically desirable. Without
party unity, Johnson would, for example, likely
experience the same sorts of problems in moving to
higher political office that Rayburn experienced in the
early 1940s. Within weeks, his Democratic liberal
allies in the fight against Shivers were excluded from
the Democratic state convention. Theoretically, no
matter how badly this wing of the party was treated,
they had to stay within the Democratic Party. Unlike
the conservative Democrats, the liberals could not turn
to the Republican Party since they were virtually
nonexistent in that party. The liberals were no match
for the factions in the party led by the new governor,
Price Daniel, Senator Johnson, and Speaker Rayburn.
Daniel had been disloyal to the party in 1952, but he
assured Rayburn of his loyalty in 1956 and claimed his
disloyalty in 1952 was solely due to the tidelands
issue. The result was an alienated liberal wing of the

Democratic Party which created innumerable problems for
Johnson and other conservative or moderate Democrats in
later years. The liberals were vocal, refused to vote
for conservative Democrats, and sometimes voted for
Republicans over conservative Democratic candidates.
From Rayburn´s perspective, however, it was the first
time that he was one of those in control of the state
Democratic Party (073, 074, 160, 161, 164, 181).

At the 1956 Democratic Convention, Rayburn did
something that puzzled observers. Adlai Stevenson got
the Democratic nomination for the Presidency and,
instead of choosing a vice-presidential running mate,
allowed the convention to choose his running mate.
Although there were a number of candidates, two of the
leading candidates were John Kennedy of Massachusetts
and Estes Kefauver of Tennessee. Rayburn did not have
a high opinion of either man. He had known Kennedy as
a member of the House and had concluded that Kennedy
was not conscientious in his work. He considered
Kefauver, an unusually colorful personality, a
maverick. Of the two men, he preferred Kennedy (033,
039). Yet during the convention, instead of
recognizing a pro-Kennedy delegation, he recognized
Tennessee which began the bandwagon of delegation vote
changes for Kefauver. Kennedy forces wondered if they
had been misled and if Rayburn was a Kefauver man. It
has been claimed that shouts from the floor of the
convention misled Rayburn and Parliamentarian Clarence
Cannon into believing that Tennessee had switched from
Gore to Kennedy. When Rayburn recognized Tennessee, he
was stunned to hear the delegation announce its switch
to Kefauver (033). Rayburn´s explanation was simply
that he saw Tennessee´s demand for recognition and saw
no one else. What is not generally known is that
Rayburn in 1956 suffered a sudden and dramatic loss of
vision. That loss was a progressive one so that in the
last years of his life, he was nearly blind (039, 136,
171). It seems highly likely, given the circumstances,
that he would have seen Tennessee´s delegation rather
than the others because it was seated directly in front
of the podium from which Rayburn presided.

Rayburn kept quiet about his vision problems. In
politics it is important to project an image of
strength. Near blindness could be interpreted as a
sign of old age and might encourage political
opposition. Rayburn depended increasingly upon his
staff to read to him. He became dependent upon friends
to identify others in the district and upon the members
of the Parliamentarian´s office to help him identify
Congressmen demanding recognition. He learned to
identify people by their voices. He did not announce
his ailment or even discuss it with friends (136).

Although Johnson and Rayburn were major figures in control of the Democratic Party in Texas, Eisenhower still carried the state. Shivers was out of power and for Rayburn that was satisfying. Price Daniel cooperated with Rayburn and Johnson, and, although Rayburn was initially distrustful of Daniel due to his earlier party disloyalty, the three men found that they could work well together (136). Daniel had given up his seat in the U.S. Senate in order to become governor and liberal Democrat Ralph Yarborough had won election to the Senate in a race for Daniel's old seat. Yarborough and Johnson worked poorly together due to their personalities and due to their different bases of political support. Yarborough reflected a far more liberal wing of the Democratic Party than Johnson did. Rayburn, although he was frequently irritated by the uncooperative nature of the liberals in the Democratic Party, generally got along well with Yarborough (025, 084, 136). However, Rayburn was unable to understand why Yarborough was unwilling to do Johnson's bidding. He seemed to assume that others would support Johnson's ambitions as he did. Nevertheless, Rayburn, appreciated Yarborough for being loyal to the Democratic Party. Having been branded a liberal himself, he seemed to tolerate Yarborough's populist impulses far more than Johnson (017, 084, 136).

Political thorns remained in Rayburn's life even though his role in the state was never stronger. Bruce Alger, for example, was elected to the U.S. House of Representatives from Dallas in 1954. Alger was a Republican and was quite conservative, but it was his style which most irritated Rayburn. He bristled when Alger told the press after a meeting that Rayburn put political party above his country (210). It was claimed that Rayburn decided as a result of Alger's statement that he would not cooperate on any government program which was of benefit to Bruce Alger (035, 036, 066, 081). Rayburn claimed that he would prefer defeating Alger over any other ten Republicans. When he was asked to generate support of leading Dallas citizens for Barefoot Sanders, the 1958 Democratic opponent of Alger's, Rayburn readily agreed and promised to try to get every leading citizen to endorse Sanders (170). Sanders, however, was unable to defeat Alger and it was not until after Alger left Congress and a Democrat was elected in his stead that Dallas was able to obtain its long desired and greatly needed Federal Building (066).

The Dallas Morning News was one of the leading papers in Texas and had very conservative editorial views. For years it had been critical of the

Democratic Party and of Rayburn. That paper's position did not change during Rayburn's lifetime, although it was disturbing to him since the <u>News</u> was received throughout his district. At times he and his friends would campaign against the <u>News</u>, noting that it was a big city Republican paper which did not have the interests of the people of Rayburn's district at heart (136). In 1952, several of his close associates became so angry with the <u>News</u> that they purchased a full page advertisement which said,

> Now...Mr. Dallas News, we know you send a lot of papers up in our district, and we read them; but...your editorial page always runs a little askew.... And somehow or other you always take a swipe at our SAM, then. Last Friday, only one day before the election, you tried to throw a "hooker" but you missed the plate.... In that last-minute editorial you said: "Mr. Rayburn represents Washington. He represents Truman. He represents New York and Michigan and Massachusetts. But he no longer represents Texas...." [We] wish you would quit sending delegations up to Bonham and quit telephoning up here so much every time he comes home, asking for his help for some pet project. We'd like for him to be able to rest a little when he comes down on vacation...but we'll bet Sam does it anyway... (028, p. 211).

That advertisement did not change the <u>News</u>, but it did appear to provide satisfaction to Rayburn's friends who believed the <u>News</u>' treatment of Rayburn was biased against him.

Bitterness remained between conservative Democrats and Rayburn. To Rayburn's satisfaction, Congressman Wingate Lucas of Ft. Worth was defeated for the Democratic nomination by Jim Wright. Rayburn felt that Lucas was only nominally a Democrat and that his views and his votes were with the Republicans. After Lucas saw such comments by Rayburn in the press (173), he began a campaign to keep Rayburn's nephew, Robert Bartley, from being reappointed to the Federal Communications Commission (174). Bartley was very close to Rayburn. He had worked as Rayburn's administrative assistant and had been a trusted political advisor (005, 030). One of the ways that Rayburn could have been deeply hurt was for Bartley to be denied renomination to the FCC, a commission in which Rayburn had a special interest since he had been House sponsor of the initial FCC legislation during the

New Deal. Eisenhower reappointed Bartley in spite of
Wingate Lucas´ attack on Bartley, no doubt feeling that
Rayburn´s friendship was more important than was the
defeated Lucas´. Rayburn did write Eisenhower and
pointed out that reappointing Bartley was the best
thing that Eisenhower could have done for Rayburn
(208).

During Eisenhower´s second administration, the
relationship between Johnson and Rayburn continued to
be strong; they continued to protect Texas interests;
and they continued to try to reach accommodations with
the Eisenhower Administration rather than to engage in
confrontations. In 1956-57, they made efforts in the
area of civil rights. Rayburn had never supported
civil rights legislation. His district, as was clearly
evident in the difficulties he had in 1948 with
Democratic primary opposition from G.C. Morris, would
not tolerate it. Additionally, early in his career he
had held traditionally Southern attitudes about race
(136). By 1956, however, he favored voting rights
legislation for blacks both on moral grounds and
because it was good for the Democratic Party (002,
058). Politically, it was legislation supported by the
liberal wing of the Democratic Party, and it would
benefit the party outside the South. With Rayburn´s
support, the civil rights forces passed the bill in the
House in 1956. The bill was not passed in the Senate
in 1956, but it did repass the House in 1957 and also
passed in the Senate. The 1957 Civil Rights Act was the
first civil rights legislation since Reconstruction
(009). Although some criticized the legislation as
being inadequate, one effect of the law was to make
Johnson appear sufficiently non-Southern to be
seriously considered as a candidate for the Presidency.

With the Democratic landslide in the 1958
Congressional elections, Rayburn was faced with
increasing pressure from northern liberals, and he
appeared less masterful as a leader than in the past
(051). Northern liberals pushed for changes in the
organization of the House, especially changes in the
powerful, conservative-dominated House Committee on
Rules. Although Rayburn rejected these requests from
the liberal wing of the party, the change in Republican
leadership from Joe Martin to Charles Halleck made it
less likely that he could depend upon any Republican
support in that committee´s voting (039). The
Democratic Party´s National Chairman, Paul Butler, also
kept up the criticism of Rayburn and his protege,
Lyndon Johnson, for their cooperation with the
Eisenhower Administration (086, 158). With a
Presidential election in 1960, Eisenhower retiring from

office, Charles Halleck as the new Republican leader, and with the split widening between liberals and conservatives within the Democratic Party, Rayburn was faced with increasing problems in leading the House. Alliances between Republicans and conservative Democrats and numerous vetoes of legislation by Eisenhower made it difficult for any Democratic initiatives to succeed. While Rayburn took an active role in promoting and opposing legislation, he frequently met with failure. The Landrum-Griffin bill, for example, was an anti-labor bill prepared as an Administration measure responding to disclosures of labor racketeering. Rayburn opposed the legislation. It was hostile to an interest that had long supported the Democratic Party, and Rayburn saw the bill as too punitive against organized labor. In spite of his intense opposition, the measure was approved overwhelmingly by both the House and by the Texas delegation in the House. Rayburn felt betrayed, believing Lyndon Johnson had aided passage of the bill and that members of the House who were his friends had refused to help him (039).

THE ELECTION OF JOHN F. KENNEDY

Rayburn did not have long to grieve over his defeat in the House. Johnson was still his protege in spite of their disagreement over labor legislation, and a Presidential election was imminent. Johnson hoped that he could win the Presidency by relying on his and Rayburn's contacts in the Congress. He did not seem to understand that members of Congress do not necessarily control their states' party convention delegates. He was half-hearted about his Presidential campaign. He showed unwillingness to get out of Washington and to campaign for the Presidency. Although Rayburn did urge him to organize a campaign and to make a more serious effort to gain the nomination, neither man seemed able to mount an adequate campaign for Johnson. Johnson's peculiar reluctance to be decisive in matters involving his career was costly to his chances to capture the nomination (081).

The Johnson forces were particularly fearful of Kennedy money and felt that Kennedy had virtually unlimited resources (082). The Johnson forces, on the other hand, could draw upon the enormous resources available to Johnson among the rich in Texas. In 1957, for example, Harold Jinks, who worked for the Democratic National Committee, wrote about Texas oil men and about the possibility of obtaining funds from

them. He wrote that he had frequently discussed the
possibility of getting campaign funds from Texas
oilmen. To his surprise, he had discovered that the
chances of getting funds were quite good. Some of the
oil men were embarrassed that Texas had not contributed
its share of money to the Democratic Party. Several
people had expressed the belief that Senator Johnson
and Speaker Rayburn were the key figures in a Texas
fund raising effort and that they could easily generate
large contributions. Jinks wrote that he shared that
opinion (169).

In 1960, Rayburn was sufficiently confident about
his fund raising abilities that he promised Texas´
$54,000 debt to the Democratic National Committee would
be paid prior to the Democratic national convention in
Los Angeles (168).

Both Rayburn and Johnson had for years protected the
oil depletion allowance which was a boon to Texas oil
men. Rayburn was known to insure that supporters of
the oil depletion allowance always had a majority on
the tax writing House Ways and Means Committee (015).
In that way he could keep legislation hostile to the
oil depletion allowance from ever coming to the floor
where it would have almost certainly passed. Both
Johnson and Rayburn had also worked to resolve the
title problems in the tidelands dispute, and both had
worked to pass natural gas deregulation legislation.
Such legislation benefited Texas and disproportionately
benefited oil and gas men (035). These wealthy
individuals showed their support of Johnson and Rayburn
in a number of ways. When Allan Shivers considered
redistricting Rayburn´s district to punish Rayburn for
his hostility to Shivers and his Shivercrat movement,
oil and gas men made it clear that Rayburn´s district
should be protected (039). Some oil men, like Hugh Roy
Cullen, could not abide the New Dealism of Rayburn.
Many others, however, were more pragmatic. Rayburn,
and to a much lesser extent Johnson as a U.S. Senator,
might have New Deal values, but they protected oil and
gas interests and so they were supported (167).
Johnson knew that large amounts of oil and gas money
could fill his campaign coffers. Both Rayburn and
Johnson had for years obtained campaign funds from oil
and gas men. Johnson had used the money for his
campaigns and for the national Democratic Party.
Rayburn needed little campaign money, and thus he used
the money to provide funds to loyal Congressmen who
needed money to support their reelection efforts (017,
058). Tip O´Neill claimed that Rayburn sent cash
contributions of $1,000 or $2,000 to loyal Congressmen
for their campaigns. On one occasion, O´Neill reported

that Rayburn gave one Congressman $10,000 (071).
O'Neill claimed that Rayburn kept a box in his office
into which lobbyists would place cash. That money was
then given by Rayburn to Democratic Congressmen who
were up for reelection (090). Former Congressman Walter
Moeller recalled that when he was up for reelection to
the House of Representatives, he received a letter from
Rayburn with $1,000 in it (176). Dwayne Little made
similar claims in his research on Sam Rayburn.
Claiming that both Rayburn and McCormack tried to give
money to needy Congressional candidates, he wrote, "It
was not uncommon for Rayburn to have $50,000 to $75,000
contributed by his influential associates in his desk
[sic] to divide among House members as the Speaker
desired" (058, pp. 127-128). Correspondence between
Sam Rayburn and John McCormack suggests that they gave
amounts of $100, $250 or more to favored Congressmen
who were up for reelection (118, 119, 120, 121, 206).
Additionally, Lyndon Johnson had the longstanding
support of George and Herman Brown of the Brown & Root
construction firm. These men bankrolled much of
Johnson's political career and as Johnson progressed on
the national scene, so did their company (017).
Ultimately, it was the superior organization of the
Kennedy forces and John Kennedy's campaign skills that
won the nomination for Kennedy.

Kennedy turned to Johnson for the Vice-Presidency.
Stories about the 1960 vice-presidential decision
abound, and numerous persons claim to have been part of
that decision (182, 186). Interpretations of the
decision vary greatly. What is known is that Kennedy
asked Johnson to be Vice-President, and Johnson sought
Rayburn's approval. What Rayburn believed is unclear.
One interpretation is that Rayburn tried to prevent
Johnson from accepting Kennedy's offer, and Hale Boggs,
a Congressman from Louisiana, who was very close to
Rayburn and was a strong Kennedy supporter, convinced
Rayburn that Kennedy could not win without Johnson on
the ticket. If Johnson was not on the ticket,
according to this story, Boggs told Rayburn that it
would be Rayburn's fault that Richard Nixon would be
elected President. Rayburn did ultimately acquiesce in
Johnson's decision to join the ticket (007, 008, 161).
Johnson, however, alienated many supporters by agreeing
to join the ticket. The Kennedy-Johnson ticket only
carried Texas by a narrow margin, although Johnson did
not need the special legislation passed by the Texas
legislature which allowed him to run for the Senate in
1960 as well as for the Vice-Presidency (184).

Rayburn had doubts about a Catholic's chances of
winning the Presidency, doubts which were dispelled

when Kennedy met with Protestant ministers in Houston and argued that his Catholicism should not disqualify him for the Presidency (136).   Rayburn, a Primitive Baptist himself, claimed that Kennedy ate the ministers "blood raw" (182, pp. 192-193).   In spite of his doubts about the Kennedy candidacy, Rayburn became an ardent Kennedy supporter and was an active campaigner in his behalf (136).

The House Committee on Rules had been a stumbling block for progressive legislation for many years (078). Rayburn had been able to use his personal influence with its conservative members and get it to report rules on some of this legislation.   His personal friendship with the arch-conservative Georgian Eugene Cox had for years been the linchpin of his relationship with the committee.   In spite of Cox´s extremely conservative views, if Rayburn told him that he needed a bill to be reported by the committee, Cox would generally try to cooperate with Rayburn, and Cox had great influence with other Southern conservatives on the committee (025).   With Cox´s death in 1952, leadership of the conservative Democratic wing of the Committee shifted to Howard Smith of Virginia.   Smith shared the same extremely conservative views as Cox, but he did not have the same close personal relationship with Rayburn.   Although both men claimed to be friends (057), Smith had supported O´Connor over Rayburn in the majority leadership fight of 1936 (130), and that support seemed symbolic of the underlying tension in their relationship.   Rayburn´s other source of support on the committee had been his relationship with Joe Martin, the Republican leader, who would tolerate liberal Republican support of committee rules favorable to Democratic legislation.   With Halleck as the Republican leader, however, Rayburn was faced with a less friendly Republican leader, one far more cunning, far more partisan, and more conservative (083).   The two moderate Republicans left the committee and were replaced by two conservative Republicans who would cooperate with Howard Smith.   Rayburn recognized that the committee would be likely to hinder the new Administration, and he decided to support action against the Committee.   Initially, Rayburn endorsed the removal of William Colmer, Smith´s closest ally, from the committee.   That proposal seems to have been a ploy to encourage support for a more moderate proposal, increasing the size of the Committee on Rules. Congressman Carl Vinson, a close friend of Rayburn who was second to Rayburn in seniority in the House, had the respect of conservative Democrats from the South. He promised Southern Democratic votes for Rayburn to expand the size of the committee as long as seniority was respected, and Colmer was not purged from the committee. It was the wedge that Rayburn had been seeking. He endorsed the compromise (039, 065).

Nevertheless, the battle over increasing the size of the committee was one of the toughest in which Rayburn was involved. Some Congressmen who promised to support the Vinson compromise reneged on their promises. Additionally, expansion of the committee required a vote by the entire House rather than by the Democratic Caucus as would have been the case with the removal of Colmer. Halleck attempted to align Republican votes with Smith´s conservative Democrats to block the committee´s expansion. Fearing that he did not have sufficient votes, Rayburn made personal appeals to his friends and delayed action on the measure. Finally, when the Rules Committee issue came up for a vote, Rayburn won by only five votes. Rayburn´s victory margin included the votes of twenty two Republicans who broke party ranks to support the committee expansion (039, 065). By any reckoning it was a close victory, one in which the Kennedy Administration got involved in spite of Rayburn´s earlier view that it was not an executive matter, but solely a matter for the House. Increasing the size of the committee did not destroy its power, the committee balance between liberals, moderates, and conservatives was a close one even with its increased size. It was instead the beginning of a decade long reduction in antagonism between the leadership of the Democratic Party in the House and the committee (024).

ILLNESS AND DEATH

As Rayburn, at 79 years of age, savored his Rules Committee victory, he began to suffer from severe back pain, pain that physicians could not explain. He was also disoriented. It had been his practice to take lengthy walks in the area around the Capitol. In the last year of his life, he got lost on at least two occasions and had to be assisted back to the Capitol. He had some difficulty in getting up and had to be helped from the Speaker´s chair on two occasions (136). He put on a brave front, saying that his back pain was nothing other than a bad case of lumbago (002). Yet, members of his staff realized that there were times when the pain was excruciating. When he was alone with members of his staff, tears would flow due to his pain. His chauffeur became so alarmed over his health that instead of dropping Rayburn off at the Anchorage Apartments and driving to his own home, he would walk with Rayburn into the apartment and stay until Rayburn went to sleep. Rayburn didn't ask that of the chauffeur, and it was against their long-established practice, but Rayburn never complained of the violation of routine (057). As the spring of 1961 wore on, Rayburn, who had always had a good appetite, lost his taste for most food and began increasingly to limit his diet. Finally, he left Washington on August 31, 1961, and went to Bonham. He claimed it was to recuperate, but some of his friends realized that he was going home to die (039, 081, 136).

In Bonham, he continued to be in pain, his appetite continued to lessen, and his personal physician began to suspect cancer. For a while, he was able to keep in touch with matters in Washington, visit with constituents and aid them with their problems, and meet with reporters (178). When his condition worsened, his physician sent him to Baylor Hospital in Dallas. There Rayburn was diagnosed as having cancer of the pancreas and it was inoperable. He returned to Bonham and went to his personal physician's private hospital. During much of that time, he was in a coma, although from time to time, he would receive guests or ask to be allowed to go to his house. Finally, he lapsed into a coma from which he did not waken. He died on November 16, 1961 (039).

Sam Rayburn's funeral in Bonham was attended by thousands. His body lay in state prior to the funeral at the Sam Rayburn Library, and long lines formed there of persons who wished to pay their last respects. Among the guests at the funeral were small farmers and businessmen from the district, Congressmen, Senators, Cabinet members, and Presidents Truman, Eisenhower, Kennedy, and Vice-President Johnson (025). He was buried in the family cemetery plot at Willow Wild Cemetery in Bonham. Appropriate to the simplicity of his life style is a small grave marker with the name "Mr. Sam." Above the name is carved a small gavel.

At the time of Rayburn's death, his old fishing friend, former brother-in-law, former Congressman, then Court of Claims Judge Marvin Jones said, "Sam wasn't a meteor, he was a star" (001). It was a fitting statement on the end of an extraordinary political career.

CONCLUSION

Tip O'Neill claimed in his memoirs that "all politics is local" (071, p. 26). That statement is a useful beginning for understanding Rayburn's lengthy political career. For a quarter of a century, Sam Rayburn was a national player on the political scence. Many times, he represented the interests of the national political party, even though his district held far more conservative, Southern values (109, 136). In part, Rayburn's decision to be a national Democrat and to lead the national Democrats explains his problems in the Democratic primaries, especially in the 1940s. Rayburn, however, was able to survive. In his entire political career, he never lost an election, nor was he even forced into a run-off election in the Democratic primary. That ability to balance national party interests with district interests is an important part of his success. He was very sensitive to his district. He made an effort to know people and to keep in touch with people in the district; he maintained an effective political network; he identified with his constituents and was accessible to them; and he brought numerous projects to the district. He benefited from having a district that had no party competition. As a result, while conservative Democrats could pose a problem for him; Republicans never created any problem in his district. The district was also grossly malapportioned and small enough so that Rayburn knew most of the extended families within the district (136).

Today, it would be much harder for a Rayburn to survive on the political scene. Increasingly, it is hard for Southern Democratic Congressmen to escape Republican opposition. More importantly, Supreme Court decisions have made small districts like Rayburn's an impossibility. Yet, future party leaders should keep in mind the advice of Tip O'Neill that, "All politics is local" (071, p. 26). A Congressman who takes care of his constituents and of local interests will be granted by those constituents the political flexibility to function on the national political scene.

At the national level, Rayburn was able to work closely with presidents, even Republican President Eisenhower. One reason for that was his reputation for rock-ribbed integrity. Another was his quiet nature. He was not one to leak news. Nor did he see every disagreement with presidents as fodder for the front page. Many times, disputes he had with presidents were privately aired; Rayburn would never be defined as a publicity hound. When, for example, he felt it was necessary to oppose President Truman's civil rights program, he did it with the minimum amount of publicity necessary to ward off the Democratic primary threat by G. C. Morris. He chose cooperation with not only the presidents of his own party, but also with Eisenhower who, he felt, was so popular that it was unwise for

Democrats to show much hostility toward him. That stance of cooperation rather than confrontation apparently made Rayburn more a part of the policy making team of the administration in power than if he had chosen a more confrontational style. President Truman saw Rayburn as so much a part of the administration team that he invited him to Cabinet meetings, an effort at cooperation that was even too much for Rayburn. Rayburn's cooperative style did not damage the Speakership. To the contrary, as Randall Ripley assessed Rayburn, he had the reputation of an "incomparable legislative wizard when faced with unfavorable odds" (077, pp. 92-93).

Part of that legislative ability was his sense of the House of Representatives. He was there so long and he knew it so well that he claimed he could feel the mood of the House (025). O'Neill has argued that Rayburn knew relatively few members of the House other than the senior committee chairs (071). Rayburn, however, claimed he knew every member of the House, and one broadcaster claimed Rayburn talked to as many as one hundred members of the House in a day (028). However he gained his knowledge, Rayburn had the necessary Congressional leadership skills to be able to sense the mood of the House (065).

Rayburn's lengthy tenure is rare in the Congressional process; only Carl Vinson of Georgia served longer in the House than Rayburn did. That lengthy tenure offered him a perspective and a kind of legislative sixth sense that was invaluable for him as a political leader. His prestige in the House in his later years was such that, as Ripley has pointed out, he was a leader in control who consulted with others, but only on his own terms (077). Rayburn served in the House at a time when seniority was still a highly respected norm, when there remained great respect for the traditions of the House, and when Congressmen were not as divided as they are today by numerous regional, ethnic and other caucuses. Rayburn worked through informal contacts. He was a product of a mentor-protege system where he learned politics from senior political leaders such as John Nance Garner. As he advanced to senior status in the House, he relied heavily on his network of youthful proteges like Carl Albert, Hale Boggs, and Richard Bolling. The large number of factional organizations in the House, the decline of the seniority system, and the decline in respect for tradition would likely make that style unworkable today.

Rayburn was a rural Southerner. His father was a Confederate war veteran; he was a segregationist; and he was dedicated to improving the lives of farmers. Yet, he was also a supporter of the New Deal, the Fair Deal, and the New Frontier. Those characteristics made him able to appeal to the two great divisions of the Democratic Party--its northern and its southern factions. Rayburn´s strength was that at a time of great regional division within the Democratic Party, he was able to be a bridge between those differences (065).

Rayburn was able to bridge other differences as well. He was able, along with Lyndon Johnson, to bridge the differences between the social welfare policies pursued by the Democratic Party and the ideological conservatism of Texas´ wealthy oil men. Although Texas oil men from time to time rebelled, many were willing to provide money to the Democratic Party even though they were philosophically opposed to the party´s programs. That was possible because Rayburn and Johnson, the leaders of the Democratic Party in Congress, protected the interests of the oil industry with the oil depletion allowance and they supported the industry position on the tidelands and on the deregulation of natural gas.

One notable characteristic of Rayburn, one noted and stressed by Caro, was his persistence (017). He made up his mind to focus on a career in the House of Representatives and to become its Speaker, and he continued moving toward that goal for decades. After he decided in 1922 that he would not run for the U.S. Senate, he clearly directed his energies toward advancement in the hierarchy of the House of Representatives, ultimately achieving his goal in 1940. Years later, Rayburn spoke with Congressman Lloyd Bentsen and thought he was offering encouragement to him. Praising Bentsen, Rayburn said that he was able, successful as a representative, and from a safe district. He advised Bentsen that in twenty years he would have a chance to be Speaker. To Rayburn, that was a reasonable goal toward which a Congressman such as Bentsen should strive; to Bentsen twenty years was an extraordinary amount of time to spend, particularly since the Speakership was not assured after that effort (006). Yet, that unusual persistence toward his goal was necessary to gain the Speakership, and it was that persistence that caused Rayburn to achieve his dream.

One further concluding point should be made about Rayburn. As Bolling pointed out in contrasting Rayburn and Garner, there was stretch to Rayburn´s mind (011, 217). He was not an ideologue. Politically, he was very flexible. He had to be to survive in the positions he was in over a half century of American politics.   During his career, he supported the New Freedom, became a leading supporter of John Nance Garner, then he was one of the Congressional workhorses of the New Deal, was Speaker during World War II, supported Truman, worked with Eisenhower, supported Johnson for President in 1960, and then supported John F.   Kennedy's New Frontier.   Although he was a southerner and a segregationist and had never before supported civil rights legislation, he was able to see a moral need and political value in the 1957 Civil Rights Act.   Without Rayburn's support, that legislation could not have passed the House (009). While that sense of pragmatism in Rayburn has been criticized (021); it shows him as a man who could accommodate change and as one who could successfully deal with change.   That characteristic within Rayburn should not be underestimated.   Indeed, it is what distinguishes him from a Congressman such as Howard Smith of Virginia, a man who could not accommodate change and who became one of the great obstructionists in Congress as a result of that inability (024).

2

Works about Rayburn

GENERAL WORKS ABOUT SAM RAYBURN AND HIS TIMES

001. ABC News. "Tribute to Sam Rayburn," 17 November 1961, Sam Rayburn Library.

On the evening of Sam Rayburn's death, ABC News broadcast this tribute which surveyed Rayburn's life. During part of the survey, various persons associated with Rayburn spoke briefly. Marvin Jones was one of those who spoke and he offered his assessment at that time. This film is valuable in providing a brief overview of the highpoints in Rayburn's life.

002. Albert, Carl. Interview with Author, 6 December 1979, Sam Rayburn Library.

Carl Albert was not only one of Rayburn's Congressional proteges, he represented the district in Oklahoma which was north of Rayburn's district. In this interview, he discussed Rayburn's sensitivity to his district, Rayburn's role in selecting him as Majority Whip, and Rayburn's views on civil rights. Albert believed that although Rayburn was a national Democrat, he was unusually responsive to constituency views in his southern, rural, conservative district. As a result, Rayburn was very concerned about the civil rights issue. He was not willing to publicly support civil rights until the struggles over the 1957 Civil Rights Act. At that time, Rayburn took the position that support for civil rights was both good for the Democratic Party and that it was morally right. Even in reference to the 1957 Civil Rights Act, however, it should be noted that Rayburn was not highly visible in the struggle outside of the House of Representatives. In reference to President Gee, Albert noted that he had asked Rayburn why he didn´t get Gee fired since he felt Rayburn could have easily done so. Rayburn claimed that it would not be worth the trouble since it would lead to much criticism of his action.

003. Bain, Richard C. <u>Convention Decisions and Voting Records</u>. Washington, D.C.: The Brookings Institution, 1960, pp. 219-224.

This is an extremely useful reference book for information on the decisions and events at all the Presidential nominating conventions. For the 1924 convention, it notes that the three week deadlock resulted in the compromise choice of John W. Davis who, of course, ran from a demoralized party base and ran dismally against Calvin Coolidge in spite of the scandals of the Harding Administration.

004. Barkley, Alben. <u>That Reminds Me</u>. New York: Doubleday, 1954, pp. 27, 99.

Barkley´s unrevealing memoir is most disappointing. A man such as Barkley, in the thick of major political issues in the House, Senate, and as Vice President, should have provided significant insights into the political process. Instead, Barkely, known as a great storyteller, contents himself with telling some of those political tales. He does, however, mention his great friendship with Sam Rayburn, calling him "my lifelong personal and political friend" (p. 99).

005. Bartley, Robert. Interview with Author, 6 January 1982, Sam Rayburn Library.

Bartley, a nephew of Rayburn, helped with his campaigns, worked as his administrative assistant, and became an FCC commissioner. He discussed some of his work as Rayburn´s administrative assistant and the organization of Rayburn´s Washington office. He also discussed some of Sam Rayburn´s political campaigns and some of the political supporters and opponents of Rayburn. In the course of this discussion, he mentioned the role of various family members, including himself, in the campaigns.

006. Bentsen, Lloyd. Interview with Author, 18 June 1980, Sam Rayburn Library.

This brief interview discusses Texas politics in the 1940s and 1950s and Rayburn´s role in Democratic Party struggles. Bentsen notes that Rayburn was very helpful to him when he was a young Texas Congressman and that Rayburn tried to encourage him to make a career of the House of Representatives. In the process of trying to offer encouragement to Bentsen, Rayburn urged him to seek the Speakership in about twenty years. Rayburn never seemed to understand that such a tentative, long-term goal would not be seen as an attractive goal for Bentsen.

007. Boggs, Hale. Interview with T. H. Baker, 13 March 1969, Lyndon Baines Johnson Library.

Boggs was one of Rayburn´s lieutenants in the House of Representatives and would have succeeded Carl Albert as Speaker had he not died in an Alaskan plane crash. While much of this interview deals with Boggs´ relationship with Lyndon Johnson, Boggs does mention that Rayburn told him he would like to be Vice President on the ticket with Stevenson in 1956.

008. Boggs, Lindy. Interview with Author, 12 June 1980, Sam Rayburn Library.

Lindy Boggs, widow of Hale Boggs (007), succeeded her husband as a New Orleans Congressperson. She knew Rayburn well and provides insights into his personality and his relationship with the Boggs family. Although she was not present when Rayburn told her husband that he would like to be the 1956 Democratic nominee for Vice President, her husband later told her of the conversation with Rayburn and expressed surprise that Rayburn would have such a desire.

009. Bolling, Richard. <u>House Out of Order</u>. New York: Dutton, 1965, pp. 174-194.

This book is a superb treatment of the House of Representatives by a House insider. Of particular value is his discussion of the 1957 Civil Rights Act and Rayburn´s attitude and behavior in reference to this legislation. Rayburn, according to Bolling, was worried about the response of his district to his support of civil rights legislation. However, he worked quietly behind the scenes to secure its passage.

010. _____. Interview with Author, 26 June 1980, Sam Rayburn Library.

>   Bolling, one of Rayburn´s closest proteges in the House of Representatives, was a Congressman from Missouri. He served on the Rules Committee and represented the interests of the Democratic leadership on that committee. He also served as liason for Rayburn with the liberal wing of the Democratic Party. Bolling worked closely with Rayburn on labor legislation, Rules Committee matters, and the 1957 Civil Rights Act. He summarizes that relationship in this interview.

011. _____. <u>Power in the House</u>. New York: E. P. Dutton, 1968, pp. 145-151.

>   Bolling, an influential member of the House of Representatives for many years, examined the powerful leaders of the House. As an intimate of Rayburn, Rayburn´s thoughts are frequently represented in this book. Of considerable value is the discussion of the alliance between Garner and Rayburn along with an interesting treatment of their personalities. Garner is described as being "very hard--even brutal"; whereas, Rayburn is described as having "greater stretch to his mind than Garner".

012. Boyd, Roland. Interview with Author, 22 May 1980, Sam Rayburn Library.

>   Boyd was a close political ally and personal friend of both Sam Rayburn and Lyndon Johnson. He was one of Rayburn´s political leaders in Collin County and his interview discusses both Johnson and Rayburn, Rayburn´s character, his campaign style, Rayburn´s political organization, and the 1960 Presidential race. As one of the most influential people in the district, he was approached by people who offered money if he would oppose Rayburn. Boyd refused the offer.

013. Bradshaw, Robert. Interview with Author, 11 May 1981, Sam Rayburn Library.

>   Bradshaw, the victim of Rayburn´s wrath, was a youth from the district whom Rayburn hired as a staff member. His interview discusses Rayburn´s relationships with his staff, his constituents, and the operation of Rayburn´s offices. It is especially valuable in pointing out the strength of Rayburn´s feelings that a primary part of his

job was to serve the interests of constituents, even those constituents who had no significant political influence.

014. Brown, D. Clayton. <u>Electricity for Rural America</u>. Westport, Conn.: Greenwood, 1980.

This superb history of rural electrification discusses the importance of REA to improving the lives of rural America. Rayburn´s role in the legislation is repeatedly stressed in the book, as is the opposition of private utilities to the legislation.

015. Burleson, Omar. Interview with Author, 18 December 1979, Sam Rayburn Library.

Burleson discussed Rayburn´s relationship with Joe Martin, the Republican leader in the House. It was Rayburn who arranged for Martin to get a chauffeur and a limousine after he lost the Republican leadership in a battle with Charles Halleck. Burleson also discussed Rayburn´s relationship with the Conservative Coalition, which Burleson led for a time, and with the Democratic Study Group. Burleson believed that Rayburn at times played one group off against the other in order to achieve his policy objectives.

016. Burney, Jim. "John Nance Garner," B.A. thesis, Incarnate Word College, 1946.

The thesis is a very favorable treatment of Garner. It is valuable primarily in that it notes the close association between Champ Clark and Garner. Garner was so loyal to Clark, claims Burney, that he voted against the interests of his district in order to support Clark.

017. Caro, Robert A. <u>The Years of Lyndon Johnson: The Path to Power</u>. New York: Alfred A. Knopf, 1982.

Although the book is about Lyndon Johnson, there is a substantial amount of new material on Sam Rayburn. The book is beautifully written investigative reporting. It contains useful physical and character descriptions of Rayburn. Caro presents Johnson in a negative light; Rayburn is treated as Johnson´s opposite. The result is that Caro´s Rayburn appears to be superhuman. Caro sometimes exaggerates the weaknesses of Johnson and the strengths of Rayburn.

018. Champagne, Anthony. "The Two Roles of Sam Rayburn," East Texas Historical Journal 20(1): 3-12.

This short article, based heavily on interviews with associates of Rayburn, discusses the differences between Rayburn´s style within the district and in Washington. It emphasizes the view that Rayburn´s personal style and his character encouraged constituent affection, trust, and votes for Mr. Sam.

019. Clary, Alla D. Interview with H.W. Kamp, 12 August 1969, North Texas State University.

Clary worked as Rayburn´s secretary for forty two years. This lengthy, broad ranging interview provides useful informational tidbits about Rayburn at various points in his Congressional career. The interview includes a comment about Byrns which suggests tensions between Byrns and Sam Rayburn. Clary´s negative statements about Lyndon Johnson must be treated cautiously. Since she strongly disliked Johnson, she tends to portray Johnson in the most negative light.

020. Cooper, Joseph and David W. Brady. "Institutional Context and Leadership Style: The House from Cannon to Rayburn," American Political Science Review 75(2): 411-425.

This article is a valuable discussion of Rayburn´s leadership style which, the authors note, stressed friendship, loyalty, permissiveness, restrained partisanship, conflict reduction, informality, and avoidance of risk. It was vastly different from the leadership styles of Cannon and Reed which emphasized the authority and power of the Speakership and party leadership. Rayburn´s strength was that he exploited his informal powers in imaginative ways.

021. Daniel, Edward Oda. "Sam Rayburn: Trials of a Party Man." Ph.D. diss., North Texas State University, 1979.

Daniel persists in speculating on Rayburn´s motives to the point that Rayburn is portrayed as manipulative, self-dealing, and disloyal to his friends. By far the most negative treatment of Rayburn, it is flawed by the highly subjective nature of Daniel´s assessment and the lack of convincing evidence to support his argument.

022. Davidson, John. "The Very Rich Life of Enrico Di Portanova." <u>Texas Monthly</u>, 10 (March, 1982): 124.

This rather gossipy magazine article discusses some of the heirs to the estate of Hugh Roy Cullen. In passing, the article contains a useful biographical sketch on Cullen which includes discussion of his ultra-conservative political views.

023. Dickson, Cecil. Interview with Author, 29 June 1980, Sam Rayburn Library.

Dickson, a reporter, public relations officer, and lobbyist, was a close friend of Rayburn from 1922 until Rayburn´s death. This extremely valuable interview discusses Garner and Rayburn, Rayburn´s efforts to become Speaker, Rayburn´s problems in his district in 1922, and Rayburn´s relationship with both Franklin Roosevelt and with Harry Truman. Dickson´s recall, even for the early years, was very impressive. His closeness to Rayburn--Rayburn introduced Dickson to his wife and urged Dickson to marry her--coupled with his powers of recall make this one of the best oral histories on Rayburn.

024. Dierenfield, Bruce J. <u>Keeper of the Rules</u>. Charlottesville: The University Press of Virginia, 1987, pp. 178-205.

This biography of Congressman Howard Smith is useful in understanding the conservative, southern wing of the Democratic Party and its relationship with the Republican Party in the House of Representatives. It is also valuable in stressing the importance of the Committee on Rules as a bottleneck for progressive legislation and its role as a check on the power of Speaker Rayburn and progressive Presidents. A scholarly treatment of the fight over the expansion of the committee is offered, along with useful descriptions of conflicts between Speaker Rayburn and Rules Committee chairman, Judge Howard Smith.

025. Dorough, C. Dwight. <u>Mr. Sam</u>. New York: Random House, 1962.

The first book length biography of Rayburn, it appeared one year after his death. The book is filled with useful information on Sam Rayburn, but it is unselective in the information it presents. Thus, one is overwhelmed with irrelevant detail such as extensive geneological material on Rayburn. Although the book is intended to be a biography, more weight is placed on Rayburn at home in Bonham that on Rayburn and his impact on the policy process in Washington.

026. Douglas, William O. Go East, Young Man. New York: Dell Publishing Co., 1974, pp. 261, 271-276, 410-411.

Prior to serving on the Supreme Court, Justice Douglas served on the Securities and Exchange Commission. He mentioned the early legislation involving the Commission, discussed some of the abuses that led to the Commission, and noted that Rayburn "fathered the three basic SEC laws" and that the Commission was therefore sometimes called the Rayburn Commission. Douglas also provided a useful character sketch of Rayburn in which he described Rayburn´s political philosophy as one of "conservative populism".

027. Dugger, Ronnie. The Politician. New York: W. W. Norton, 1982.

Dugger, deeply involved in liberal Democratic politics in Texas, is not an objective observer of Lyndon Johnson. Yet, he provides useful data on Johnson´s shift from New Dealer to conservative Democrat. He also amasses impressive evidence that Johnson was reluntant to anger Shivers and was fearful of taking too active a role in the Stevenson Presidential campaign. Other parts of the book are less impressive. For example, there is an odd treatment of the Vietnam War during the Johnson years in which Dugger offers Johnson´s view of the Alamo as a cause of the war.

028. Dulaney, H.G., Edward Hake Phillips, MacPhelan Reese, eds. Speak Mr. Speaker. Bonham. The Sam Rayburn Foundation, 1978, p. 63.

This volume collects letters and speeches of Sam Rayburn and organizes them chronologically and topically in an effort to present Sam Rayburn´s attitudes and values. Not only is it a useful collection of excerpts from documents in the files of the Sam Rayburn Library, but it succeeds in presenting a good overview of Rayburn´s ideas over his lifetime. Briefly noted is a statement of Rayburn, "I think Roosevelt´s two greatest mistakes were his Supreme Court Plan in 1937 and his attempted congressional purge in 1938. Officially, I had nothing to do with either".

029. Dulaney, H.G.   Interview with Author, 15 August 1980, Sam Rayburn Library.

Dulaney worked on Rayburn´s staff for ten years and was personally very close to the Speaker. He provided a wide ranging interview on staff relations, Rayburn´s relationship with his constituents, and on Rayburn´s character. He stressed the simplicity of Rayburn´s life style and his desire to maintain close contact with his constituents. He also stressed Rayburn´s ability to identify with his poor, farming constituency.

030. Dye, Martha Rayburn.   Interview with Author, 2 December 1980, Sam Rayburn Library.

Dye, a niece of Sam Rayburn, discussed Rayburn´s relationship with his siblings and their children. She also discussed the political involvement of the family members in the Rayburn organization, especially the involvement of Dick Rayburn who was her father and Sam Rayburn´s brother.

031. Evans, Rowland, and Robert Novak.   Lyndon B. Johnson: The Exercise of Power. London: George Allen and Unwin, 1968, pp. 10, 12-13, 19, 33, 148.

This journalistic treatment of Lyndon Johnson is probably the most insightful biographical treatment of Johnson which was published prior to Robert Caro´s first volume on Johnson, The Years of Lyndon Johnson: The Path to Power (017). Numerous references are made to the "father-son relationship" that existed between Rayburn and Johnson.   Interestingly, they note that after 1955, "his long and intimate relationship with Rayburn underwent a subtle change; the younger man now became the dominant partner in the team" (p. 148). While Caro does not share that assessment, it is clear that Rayburn-Johnson was a formidable legislative team and that emphasis should be placed on their ability to work as a team.

032. Fenno, Richard F., Jr.   Home Style: House Members in Their Districts.   Boston: Little, Brown and Company, 1978.

Although this book does not explicitly refer to Rayburn, it is extremely useful as a theoretical framework to understand how Rayburn (or other Congressmen) relate to constituents. One thing Congressmen try to do is identify with the

constituents so that they are considered to be
"one of us".

033. Fontenay, Charles L. <u>Estes Kefauver: A
Biography</u>. Knoxville: University of Tennessee Press,
1980, pp. 102, 230-31, 272, 275.

This useful biography of Kefauver explains his
choice of a maverick political role and notes
Rayburn´s unfriendliness to Kefauver, in part, no
doubt, because of Kefauver´s choice of roles. Most
importantly, the book suggests that Rayburn was
misled by shouts from the floor and possibly
Parliamentarian Clarence Cannon´s misinterpre-
tation of those shouts. Rayburn mistakenly
believed that Tennessee had switched its votes
from Gore to Kennedy instead of to Kefauver.

034. Freeman, Martha. Interview with Author, 6 January
1982, Sam Rayburn Library.

Freeman, a member of Rayburn´s staff, discussed
the functioning of Rayburn´s congressional staff,
how he dealt with correspondence, and how he dealt
with visitors. Additionally, she told this
revealing story of how Rayburn responded to black
schoolchildren on a trip to Washington.

035. Green, George Norris. <u>The Establishment in Texas
Politics: The Primitive Years, 1938-1957</u>. Westport,
Conn.: Greenwood Press, 1979.

An excellent treatment of conservatism in Texas
politics, this volume notes that there was strong
support for the states rights claim by the oil
industry. Texas´ royalties were far less that the
royalties required by the federal government and
so a successful claim to the tidelands by Texas
would be a boon for the oil industry. Norris
noted correctly that there were other issues,
such as race, which affected voting in 1952;
although the tidelands issue was a very important
one which was stressed strongly by such state
leaders as Allan Shivers and Price Daniel. His
book also contains a useful discussion of one of
Rayburn´s arch-enemies, Bruce Alger, Republican
Congressman from Dallas. Alger, he notes, was
very conservative, but usually ineffective.

036. _____. "The Far Right Wing in Texas Politics,
1930s-1960s," Ph.D. diss., Florida State University,
1966, pp. 258-259.

Useful in understanding the values of the
ultra-conservatives in Texas politics from the New
Deal through the New Frontier, it also provides
valuable information on those wealthy individuals
who contributed funds to support conservative
causes. Alger was greatly admired by
ultra-conservatives for his vocal opposition to
big government and social welfare programs. He
rapidly made himself the enemy of those with
national Democratic Party sympathies, including
Rayburn.

037. Hairgrove, Kenneth Dewey. "Sam Rayburn:
Congressional Leader, 1940-1952," Ph.D. diss., Texas
Tech University, 1974.

The dissertation is of limited value. It is a
good description of much of Sam Rayburn´s career;
however, it does not contribute new information or
a new perspective on Rayburn.

038. Halberstam, David. The Powers That Be. New York:
Alfred A. Knopf, 1979, pp. 3-6.

Very little in this book deals with Rayburn;
although the important point is made that Rayburn
was very able and very old-fashioned in his
attitudes and values. Additionally, the book
notes that Rayburn traveled little outside the
United States.

039. Hardeman, D. B. and Donald C. Bacon. Rayburn: A
Biography. Austin: Texas Monthly Press, 1987.

Of the three book length biographies of Rayburn
(see, 025 and 084), Hardeman and Bacon´s is
clearly the superior work. The book benefited
greatly from Hardeman´s long and close personal
association with Rayburn; yet, it retains
objectivity. Much previously unpublished material
is presented in this carefully written volume. By
far the strongest part of the book is the
treatment of Rayburn during the Roosevelt years.
No other work has been able to capture the extent
of Rayburn´s stature as a workhorse of the New
Deal in Congress.

040. Hardeman, D. B. D.B.: Reminiscences of D.B.
Hardeman. Ed. Larry Hufford. Austin, Texas:
AAR/Tantalus, Inc., 1984.

D.B. Hardeman was a journalist, state
representative, and activist within the Democratic

Party. He was employed by Rayburn as a research
assistant, although he was primarily involved in
writing a biography of Sam Rayburn. He became a
close friend of Rayburn and came to know him very
well. This book is a collection of interviews
that Hardeman gave over the years. Although the
material ranges far beyond Sam Rayburn, useful
information about Rayburn permeates the book.

041. _____. Interview with D. Clayton Brown, August,
1969, Sam Rayburn Library.

In this wide-ranging interview with Hardeman, he
discusses Rayburn´s integrity, his finances, and
his values. Hardeman notes that Rayburn only
owned stock once, but soon sold it because he
feared a conflict of interest. Hardeman also
discusses Rayburn´s strong sense of loyalty to the
Democratic Party. Finally, Hardeman notes that
Rayburn felt a major source of funds for his
opposition were the oil interests that were
controlled by Harry Sinclair, a major figure in
the Harding Administration and the scandals of
that administration.

042. _____. "Sam Rayburn and the House of
Representatives." In The Presidency and the Congress,
edited by William S. Livingston, Lawrence Dodd, and
Richard Schatt. Austin: LBJ School, 1979.

This overview of Sam Rayburn as a Congressional
leader contains particularly useful information on
Rayburn´s character. The only stock Rayburn ever
owned was $1,000 worth of Kirby Petroleum stock
which caused him such worries over possible
conflicts of interest that he sold the stock.
Later investments by Rayburn were in land, cattle,
and U.S. savings bonds, investments which did not
cause him the worries that even a small amount of
stock had caused.

043. Hardeman, D.B.. "Unseen Side of the Man They
Called Mr. Speaker." Life, 51 (1 December 1961):21.

Great stress is placed on Rayburn´s loneliness,
his complete dedication to the House of
Representatives, and upon his quiet, private
personality. While there is much truth to this
description of Rayburn, it leads to the mistaken
inference that Rayburn led a hermit-like,
friendless life in his later years.

044. Heacock, Walter Judson. "William Brockman Bankhead: A Biography." Ph.D. diss., University of Wisconsin, 1952, pp. 163-164.

This useful biography of Speaker William Bankhead notes that Rainey had served as Speaker Garner´s Majority Leader and was chosen in part because being from Illinois, he added regional balance to party leadership.

045. Hinckley, Barbara. The Seniority System in Congress. Bloomington: Indiana University Press, 1971, p. 101-102.

In contrast to the argument that Rayburn had several tough campaigns for reelection, Hinckley argues that he was from a politically secure district. That is only the case if one looks at general elections where the Democratic nominee was certain of victory. However, if one examines competition within the Democratic primary, Rayburn had a number of tough battles for renomination.

046. Hughes, Sarah. Interview with Author, 5 February 1980, Sam Rayburn Library.

During this brief interview, Hughes mentioned that she and Rayburn campaigned together for Al Smith in 1928. The bulk of the interview discusses the help she received from Rayburn in becoming a federal district judge. Rayburn apparently got Justice Department approval for the appointment--Hughes was beyond the usual age for a judgeship--by holding up an appropriation desired by Attorney General Robert Kennedy and by having an argument with the Attorney General.

047. Ingraham, Joe and Jack Porter. Interview with Maclyn Burg, 9 November 1972, Dwight D. Eisenhower Library.

During the course of this interview, which was primarily on Republican Party politics, Jack Porter stated that he had met with Rayburn to complain about price controls. Rayburn, in turn, expressed his irritation that Hugh Roy Cullen, a friend of Porter´s, had given Morris $10,000 in 1944. Porter promised to talk with Cullen. Soon after the meeting with Rayburn, price controls were dropped and when Morris ran against Rayburn in 1948, instead of money, he received a telegram of encouragement from Cullen.

048. Jackson, Henry. Interview with Author, 12 June 1980, Sam Rayburn Library.

Jackson was closely associated with Rayburn during the time he was in the House of Representatives. He notes Rayburn´s skills in building support among Congressional colleagues by awarding them choice committee assignments and by giving them special favors such as arranging White House dinner invitations for them. He also offers a useful comparison and contrast of Rayburn and Lyndon Johnson. He notes that it was Rayburn who was clearly the most respected and most trusted of the two men; although in their very different ways, both were extremely effective as Congressional leaders.

049. James, Marquis. <u>Mr.   Garner   of   Texas</u>. Indianapolis: Bobbs-Merrill Co, 1939.

No biography of Garner is satisfactory; however, this book provides a useful description of Garner´s life. It should be read critically since the Garner of James´ book is a far more benign figure than the real John Nance Garner.

050. Johnson, Mrs. Lyndon. Interview with Author, 13 November 1979, Sam Rayburn Library.

Not only was Lyndon Johnson a close associate of Rayburn, but as Mrs. Johnson points out, Rayburn was very close to the Johnson family and frequently socialized with them. She also notes that several women were attracted to Rayburn and unsuccessfully sought to marry him.

051. Jones, Charles O. <u>The Minority Party in Congress</u>. Boston: Little, Brown and Co., 1970.

Jones examines the role of the minority in the Congress. He notes that in the House, the minority has very little opportunity to initiate policy. Rayburn is discussed briefly in this volume and is treated as a successful Congressional leader whose control over his party and over the House begins to decline in the late 1950s.

052. Jones, Marvin. Interview with Jerry N. Hess, 3, 20, 24 April, 8, 14 May 1970, Harry S Truman Library.

This lengthy, broad-ranging interview includes discussion of the strong personal friendship between Jones, who during much of Rayburn´s career was a Congressman from Amarillo, Texas, and Rayburn. Jones briefly mentions Rayburn´s marriage to his sister, Metze. Essentially, he argues that the reason for the divorce was simply that they did not get along and he notes that there was no animosity--that Rayburn sought to see her when he was dying. In another part of the interview, Jones claims that he gave the rural electrification bill to Rayburn because Rayburn had been dealing with some tough legislation and he needed legislation like the REA bill to build up his political support.

053. _____. Marvin Jones Memoirs. Ed. Joseph M. Ray. El Paso: Texas Western Press, 1973, p. 22.

Marvin Jones, having first met Rayburn in law school, was one of Rayburn´s oldest and closest Congressional friends. His memoirs note that friendship, hint at competing ambitions for leadership in the House of Representatives, and notes that they were both followers of Joe Bailey. Jones states that Bailey took an interest in both Rayburn´s and Jones´ career as long as he lived.

054. Kennon, Donald R., "John Nance Garner." In The Speakers of the U.S. House of Representatives: A Bibliography, 1798-1984, edited by Donald R. Kennon. Baltimore: Johns Hopkins Press, 1986, pp. 226-236.

This brief sketch of Garner offers a useful description of Garner´s habits, particularly his poker playing. It also provides a bibliography on Garner which is a good starting point for anyone desiring to do serious research on Garner.

055. _____. "Sam Rayburn." In The Speakers of the U.S. House of Representatives: A Bibliography, 1798-1984, edited by Donald R. Kennon. Baltimore: Johns Hopkins Press, 1986, pp. 248-260.

This brief essay on Sam Rayburn includes a valuable bibliography. It mentions Rayburn´s length of service, includes some information about positions he took, and mentions aspects of his personality. In passing, some of Rayburn´s close friends, including Hull, are mentioned.

056. Kilday, Paul J. Interview with H.W. Kamp, 28 August 1965, North Texas State University.

Kilday was an influential Texas Congressman. While little of the interview deals with Rayburn, Kilday does note that until Sam Rayburn and Ft. Worth booster Amon Carter became interested, Kilday thought he had an agreement from the air force to locate the academy in his San Antonio district.

057. Kimbrough, Rene. Interview with Author, 23 November 1980, Sam Rayburn Library.

Kimbrough, a member of Sam Rayburn´s staff, offers an excellent analysis of the operation of Rayburn´s office. She also presents useful information about Rayburn´s personality, his relationships with several political leaders such as Howard Smith, politics in the district, and information about his final illness. The number of detailed examples in this interview makes it especially valuable in understanding Rayburn and how he worked within the Washington and the Bonham political scene.

058. Little, Dwayne L. "The Political Leadership of Speaker Sam Rayburn, 1940-1961," Ph.D. diss., University of Cincinnati, 1970.

An excellent disseration on Rayburn which digs out important information on Rayburn´s marriage, some of his opposition in the district, and on his relationships with wealthy oil men. Little sees Rayburn as a power broker rather than as a politician with his own political agenda.

059. Lowry, Oscar. Interview with Author, 2 October 1981, Sam Rayburn Library.

Related to Rayburn by marriage, Lowry did Rayburn´s taxes and discussed Rayburn´s tax situation. Additionally, he discussed Rayburn´s relationship with the family. In the course of talking about the family, he mentioned the involvement of various family members in Rayburn´s political campaigns, especially the role of W. A. Thomas in the early years of Rayburn´s political career. Contrary to Hardeman and Bacon (039), who felt that Thomas gave bad advice to Rayburn, Lowry believed that Thomas was a valued member of the Rayburn political organization.

060. Martin, Joe as told to Robert J. Donovan. <u>My First Fifty Years in Politics</u>. New York: McGraw Hill, 1960, pp. 8-9.

In these unrevealing memoirs of the Republican leader of the House of Representatives and the Speaker of the House for four years, Martin discusses his close relationship with Rayburn. He argues that it was in the interests of his party for him to work closely with Rayburn. However, he also adds that there were "some who resented" their "long-close friendship."

061. May, Irvin M., Jr. <u>Marvin Jones: The Public Life of an Agrarian Advocate</u>. College Station: Texas A & M University Press, 1980.

Jones was one of Rayburn's closest friends and during the New Deal was chairman of the Agriculture Committee of the House of Representatives. Although this book does mention the friendship between Jones and Rayburn, there is little information about Rayburn or his marriage to Jones' sister. Instead, it should be read for an understanding of agriculture and agricultural policy during the New Deal. Such information is valuable in understanding Rayburn's agricultural district and Rayburn's ties to the soil.

062. McCormack, John. Interview with Author, 11 March 1980, Sam Rayburn Library.

It is clear from this interview that McCormack had great respect and personal affection for Rayburn. Although the interview was not very revealing, McCormack does describe John O'Connor and stresses that he was a difficult personality. Interestingly, McCormack did note that by 1944, he became convinced that Roosevelt's health was failing him.

063. _____. Interview with Deward Brown, 18 July 1969, Sam Rayburn Library.

In this interview, McCormack discusses his relationship with Speaker Rayburn. The most important part of the interview is McCormack's claim that he urged Rayburn to attend the 1944 Democratic convention because he felt Rayburn could get the vice presidential nomination. Rayburn told McCormack he could not attend because he was facing a tough primary battle against G.C. Morris.

064. McKay, Seth Sheppard. <u>Texas Politics, 1906-1944</u>. Lubbock: Texas Tech Press, 1952, pp. 326-327, 357-359.

This highly descriptive treatment of 38 years of Texas politics reads like a synthesis of hundreds of newspaper articles. A look at the references suggests that newspapers are the main source. It is, however, useful in showing Morris´ influence at the state level as an opponent of O´Daniel´s regressive taxation scheme.

065. MacNeil, Neil. <u>The Forge of Democracy: The House of Representatives</u>. New York: David McKay, 1963.

MacNeil has written an excellent history of the House of Representatives. Because Rayburn was such a major force in the House, he is mentioned throughout the book. MacNeil sees Rayburn as being the force that bridged a regionally and ideologically divided Democratic Party. Also of relevance is his discussion of the battle over the expansion of the House Committee on Rules and Rayburn´s strategy in that fight.

066. Miller, Dale. Interview with Author, 13 June 1980, Sam Rayburn Library.

Miller, long-time Washington lobbyist for the Dallas Chamber of Commerce, is the son of Roy Miller, an influential lobbyist and Garner ally. Miller and his wife were close social friends of Rayburn, frequently attended parties with him, and invited him to their home. The interview is also valuable in pointing to Rayburn´s relationship with Hatton Sumners and Bruce Alger, along with discussing some of Sumners´ and Alger´s eccentricities.

067. Miller, Hope Ridings. Interview with Author, 19 August 1986, Sam Rayburn Library.

Miller wrote for the "Society" pages of the <u>Washington Post</u>. She also was a magazine publisher and a well-known author. She was a close friend of Rayburn due to her father´s friendship with Rayburn and because her home town was Sherman, Texas, which was in Rayburn´s district. She spoke about Rayburn´s social life, including his female companions. Rayburn also spoke with her about his personal life and about his relationship with a widow who was a friend of Miller. Miller offers the most revealing portrait of the private life of Sam Rayburn.

068. Miller, William "Fishbait" told to Frances Spatz Leighton. <u>Fishbait: The Memoirs of the Congressional Doorkeeper</u>. Englewood Cliffs, New Jersey: Prentice Hall, 1977, p. 229.

This gossipy volume by the former Congressional doorkeeper is of minimal scholarly value. It primarily discusses the foibles and vices of members of Congress. However, Miller does note that during the time that he knew Rayburn, Rayburn was seeing a woman one or two times a week. He adds that Rayburn was loyal to her and saw no other women during this time. Although he does not mention her name, I believe this woman was the widow of a cabinet member in the Wilson Administration with whom he regularly dined in the Speaker's dining room in the Capitol (see, 136).

069. Murph, David Rupert. "Price Daniel: The Life of a Public Man, 1910-1956." Ph.D. diss., Texas Christian University, 1975, pp. 159-219.

This dissertation examines one of the major actors in the tidelands controversy and also offers an explanation of the origins of the controversy and the politics surrounding it. Daniel is treated rather uncritically, however. There is no analysis of the weaknesses of the Texas claim to the tidelands or of the likelihood that Texas would be unsuccessful in its claim. Similarly, there is no effort to compare Daniel's position on the tidelands with Rayburn's proposed compromise on this issue and to determine which position would provide greater benefit to Texas.

070. Olien, Roger M. <u>From Token to Triumph: The Texas Republicans Since 1920</u>. Dallas: SMU Press, 1982.

This is a well researched volume on the changing character of the Republican Party in Texas. Its movement from an ultra-conservative, patronage oriented party to a party that is a genuine contender for Texas political offices is well treated. As a patronage based party, of course, growth is not desirable since growth merely increases competition for patronage jobs. With the changes in leadership in the party which resulted from the success of Eisenhower in 1952, the party became growth oriented and began to make serious efforts to obtain offices.

071. O'Neill, Tip with William Novak. <u>Man of the House</u>. New York: Random House, 1987, p. 131.

These interesting memoirs of Speaker O´Neill should be read with caution since they are often self-serving. There are some errors in O´Neill´s treatment of Rayburn which make it appear that he is attempting to compare himself favorably with Rayburn. For example, he falsely claims that Rayburn only knew a small number of Democratic Congressmen and uses as evidence that Rayburn did not recognize a senior Democratic Congressman. O´Neill does not point out that Rayburn´s eyesight would have been so poor at the time that he could not have distinguished the Congressman´s facial features. O´Neill does claim, as do others (058, 136), that Rayburn gave substantial campaign contributions to loyal Democrats. O´Neill´s amounts are considerably higher than other estimates; he claims the average contribution was $2,000 and the largest was $10,000. As do others, he believes the money came from Rayburn´s Texas oil friends.

072. Parmet, Herbert S. The Democrats. New York: Macmillan, 1976, p. 118.

This useful discussion of Democratic Party politicians and politics includes some discussion of Rayburn. The treatment of Rayburn includes a discussion of the threat of redistricting Rayburn´s district by Allan Shivers. According to Parmet, Shivers could have defeated Rayburn and achieved the objective of equitable redistricting if he combined Rayburn´s Fourth Congressional district with the more populous and much more conservative suburbs of Dallas.

073. Parten, J.R. Interview with Author, 19 January 1980, Sam Rayburn Library.

Parten, a wealthy oil man and a leader in the liberal wing of the Texas Democratic Party, spoke of his friendship for Rayburn, of the factionalism within the Texas Democratic Party, and of the tidelands issue. He noted that Rayburn had checked into the economic implications of the Rayburn compromise compared to the Texas claim over the tidelands and was convinced that the Rayburn compromise would bring far more resources to Texas. He spoke little of his financial contributions to Democrats, but did remark that he had contributed money to Rayburn.

074. Phillips, William G. Yarborough of Texas. Washington, D.C.: Acropolis, 1969, pp. 42-43.

This biographical treatment of Ralph Yarborough, one of the leaders of the liberal-labor wing of the Democratic Party, asserted that Yarborough's supporters in his race against Daniel felt that the election had been stolen from Yarborough. In part because of that reason and also because of their hostility to Daniel's conservatism and his party disloyalty in 1952, they refused to cooperate with Daniel. The result was that Daniel welcomed any move to destroy their power within the state party.

075. Puett, Jimmy Dale.   "Sam Rayburn's Influence on Public Policy," M.A. thesis, East Texas State University, August, 1965, pp. 89-90.

Puett discusses the conflict with Oklahoma over the Dension Dam and claims that Rayburn, then Majority Leader, suggested to the Oklahoma delegation that if there was so much concern about protecting Oklahoma land from flooding, he would see to it that Oklahoma got no more federal money for government projects. Shortly thereafter, claims Puett, the Oklahoma legislature which had instructed its delegation to oppose the dam, withdrew its instruction.

076. Reedy, George. <u>Lyndon B. Johnson: A Memoir</u>. New York: Andrews and McMeel, Inc., 1982, pp. xi, 39-40, 157.

Reedy, for many years a Johnson staff member, offers some comments on Rayburn and an assessment of Johnson which provide valuable insights into the perceptions others had of the two men. Reedy described Rayburn as "sainted" (p. xi). He was, claimed Reedy, "a man who was deservedly legendary in his own time for integrity, selflessness, and a simple, direct love of country--virtues that are ascribed to many politicians but that fit very few I have encountered" (pp. 39-40). In describing Johnson, Reedy wrote, "As a human being, he was a miserable person--a bully, sadist, lout, and egotist. He had no sense of loyalty ... and he enjoyed tormenting those who had done the most for him" (p. 157).

077. Ripley, Randall B. <u>Party Leaders in the House of Representatives</u>, Washington, D.C.: Brookings Institution, 1967.

This general treatment of leadership in the House of Representatives treats Rayburn as the most effective of the modern House leaders.   Ripley sees Rayburn as being in control of the House and being a legislative master.

078. Robinson, James A.   The House Rules Committee. Indianapolis: Bobbs-Merrill Co., 1963.

One of the best historical treatments of the House Committee on Rules.   It traces how the committee became obstructionist and examines the efforts, including the expansion of the committee in 1961, to make the committee less of a legislative hurdle.

079. Roberts, Ray.   Interview with Author, 16 June 1980, Sam Rayburn Library.

Roberts was one of Rayburn´s political leaders in the district, a member of his staff in 1940, a state senator, and Rayburn´s successor in the House.   He provides a useful description of Rayburn´s great power which was coupled with a folksy political style and notes that in 1940, Rayburn thought Roosevelt was going to ask him to be vice president; instead, he asked Rayburn to second Wallace´s nomination for vice president.

080. Roosevelt, James.   Interview with Author, 17 May 1984, Sam Rayburn Library.

This interview concentrates on the relationship between Franklin Roosevelt, Sam Rayburn, John Nance Garner and Lyndon Johnson.   It also examines Rayburn´s relationship with the Democratic Study Group (DSG).   James Roosevelt, active in the Group, noted that Rayburn appeared to be threatened by the Group and quickly infiltrated it with his allies.   Roosevelt stressed that Rayburn had no need to feel threatened by the DSG since there was never any intention to oppose Rayburn.

081. Rutherford, J.T.   Interview with Author, 18 June 1980, Sam Rayburn Library.

Rutherford discussed Rayburn´s image in Texas.   In Dallas and in Midland, Texas, there were many community influentials, according to Rutherford, who regarded Rayburn as being too liberal. Additionally, he discussed the relationship between Lyndon Johnson and Sam Rayburn.   It was, noted Rutherford, very much like a son-father relationship.   He also commented upon Lyndon Johnson´s indecisiveness in matters relating to his political future.

082. Sanders, Barefoot. Interview with Author, 29 October 1984, Sam Rayburn Library.

Sanders discussed his campaign against Bruce Alger, Texas politics in the 1950s, and Sam Rayburn's relationship with Lyndon Johnson. He did not believe Rayburn raised much money for him in his campaign against Alger since he only raised $25,000 in the Democratic primary and another $25,000 in the general election. Alger, he noted, outspent him five to one. He also noted that he did not believe talk of redistricting Rayburn's district was serious, since Rayburn was quite influential as the Speaker and Texas would not have wanted to lose a Speaker. Additionally, there was not sympathy in the legislature for giving Dallas additional representation. In talking about the 1960 Presidential campaign, Sanders noted that to Johnson's supporters, "the Kennedy money was everywhere. I mean, they were spreading it all over the place."

083. Scott, Hugh. Interview with Author, 23 June 1980, Sam Rayburn Library.

Scott discussed his work on the House Committee on Rules when he served in the House of Representatives. He noted that Joe Martin allowed him to vote with the Democrats on the committee and never objected. Martin, he felt, was far less able as a Congressional leader than was Rayburn. However, he felt both Rayburn and Martin genuinely liked each other and worked well together. Halleck was far less tolerant of liberal Republicans than was Martin and was very aggressive and antagonistic. Scott personally did not like Halleck and felt that Rayburn had difficulty working with him.

084. Steinberg, Alfred. <u>Sam Rayburn</u>. New York: Hawthorn Books, Inc., 1975.

Less cluttered that the Dorough biography of Rayburn, it contains little material that is not already presented in Dorough's book (025). The work is highly descriptive and offers little analysis or insight into Sam Rayburn.

085. Stephenson, Charles W. "The Democrats of Texas and Texas Liberalism, 1944-1960: A Study in Political Frustration." M.A. thesis, Southwest Texas State College, 1967, p. 14.

The thesis is a useful description of the failure of the liberal wing of the Texas Democratic Party to gain power within the party. The most important aspect of the thesis for the Rayburn scholar is Stephenson´s claim, based on an interview he had with political activist Creekmore Fath, that Rayburn did not believe Truman would win in 1948.

086. Sundquist, James L. Politics and Policy: The Eisenhower, Kennedy, and Johnson Years. Washington, D.C.: The Brookings Institution, 1968, pp. 403-410.

This excellent volume, which discusses the politics surrounding several major policy issues from the Eisenhower through the Johnson years, contains a valuable discussion of liberal Democratic pressures on Rayburn and on Johnson. Unhappy with the moderate course pursued by Rayburn and Johnson during the Eisenhower years, liberal Democrats, with Paul Butler at the forefront, tried to gain a voice in Congressional policy making circles. Although Johnson initially seemed willing to grant them a voice, Rayburn successfully opposed Butler´s effort to inject non-Congressional leaders into Congressional policy making. Sundquist also discusses the liberal pressures on Rayburn and Johnson within Congress. He does note, however, that the Democratic Study Group never wished to challenge Rayburn´s authority and that it always tried to keep Rayburn informed of its activities.

087. Thompson, Frank. Interview with Author, 13 March 1986, Sam Rayburn Library.

Thompson was one of the more influential members of the liberal wing of the Democratic Party in the House. He was also on good terms with Rayburn and notes the immense respect with which Rayburn was held. Rayburn, however, would not tolerate criticism of his protege, Lyndon Johnson. When Thompson criticized Johnson, he noted that he was reprimanded and punished by Rayburn for doing so. He added that it was the only time that Speaker Rayburn ever disciplined him. Additionally, Thompson noted that once Rayburn had privately approved the germaneness of a labor-related amendment, but after Johnson spoke with Rayburn, Rayburn changed his mind and refused to allow the amendment as germane. Thompson felt that Johnson had asked Rayburn to rule the amendment out of order because it would have hurt

Brown & Root Construction Company, a major contributor to Johnson's campaigns.

088. Timmons, Bascom N. <u>Garner of Texas : A Personal History</u>. New York: Harper and Brothers, 1948.

As James' biography (049), this book presents a very benign picture of John Nance Garner and is disappointing to those looking for an objective, scholarly treatment of Garner. It does present a thorough descriptive treatment of the man and it tends to be treated as the standard biography of Garner. It should be read as a description of a controversial figure which was written by a friend of Garner.

089. Tindall, George Brown. <u>The Disruption of the Solid South</u>. Athens: University of Georgia Press, 1972, pp. 26-29.

Overall, this is a very useful book for those who wish to understand the growth of the Republican Party in the South and the decline of the Democratic Party. A brief discussion of the election of 1928 is offered. Tindall explains the strength of the Republican vote as an anti-Catholic vote; although the race issue, he argued, kept the Deep South in the Democratic fold and Arkansas' Senator Joe Robinson's candidacy for the vice presidency kept Arkansas Democratic.

090. Tolchin, Martin. "Ex-Speaker O'Neill: A Salty Par for the Course." <u>New York Times</u>, 28 August 1987, p. A 14.

This discussion of Speaker Tip O'Neill in retirement notes that in 1952, when O'Neill was elected to the U.S. House of Representatives, there was a cash box kept in Speaker Sam Rayburn's office. Lobbyists would place cash in the box and Speaker Rayburn would then give the money to Congressmen who were running for re-election. This example is used by O'Neill to illustrate the vast differences in today's campaign finance laws compared to an earlier era.

091. Tunnell, D. M. Interview with Author, 21 November 1980.

Tunnell, one of Rayburn's political leaders in Kaufman County, discussed Rayburn's political style and his dealings with Rayburn at the 1956 national Democratic convention. Tunnell also recalled Rayburn's feeling that Eisenhower played too much golf and did not work hard enough. Rayburn felt Eisenhower was far more successful in the military than in politics. However, he did not dislike Eisenhower; that dislike was reserved for Richard Nixon.

092. Wilcox, Clair. <u>Public Policies Toward Business</u>. Homewood, Illinois, 1960, pp. 629-636.

This general treatment of economic regulations includes a brief description of the Public Utility Holding Company Act and its effects. It is useful primarily in providing a short, understandable summary of the legislation.

093. Worley, Mrs. Gene. Interview with Author, 20 June 1980, Sam Rayburn Library.

Mrs. Worley is the widow of a Texas Congressman who was a very close personal friend of Rayburn. Mrs. Worley was also close to Rayburn, in part because she had family who were from Rayburn's district and were Rayburn's allies. She spoke of the frequent gatherings of the close-knit younger members of the Texas Congressional delegation. Rayburn, unlike some of the older Congressmen like Dallas Congressman Hatton Sumners, attended the gatherings, enjoyed himself, and was viewed as far younger than his years.

FROM THE EARLY YEARS TO THE NEW DEAL

094. Acheson, Sam Hanna. <u>Joe Bailey, The Last Democrat</u>. New York: Macmillan, 1932.

While it is the only book length published study of Bailey, it is not of the scholarly quality of Holcomb's dissertation (099). Nevertheless, Acheson's work has become a standard reference on Bailey. Rayburn is not treated in this book; however, it is valuable in understanding Rayburn's first mentor.

095. "Alcohol Smith's Platform." Anonymous poem printed on the church bulletin of Harry St. Methodist Episcopal Church. Joe T. Robinson Papers, The Church in Politics # 1 file, University of Arkansas.

Joe Robinson, senator from Arkansas, ran for the Vice Presidency on the ticket with Al Smith. One of his responsibilities was to deal with religious bigotry in the South. He maintained files on anti-Catholic materials that were being distributed in conjunction with the Presidential race and this poem is but one example of those materials.

096. Anders, Evan. <u>Boss Rule in South Texas</u>. Austin: The University of Texas Press, 1982.

Although this book is primarily about the political bosses who ran South Texas, it offers a useful discussion of Senator Joe Bailey in his later and more politically conservative years. It also offers the most objective treatment of John Nance Garner. Anders provides useful information on Garner's personality and political style. He concentrates on Garner in the Texas legislature and in his first few years in the House of Representatives. The work is particularly good in explaining Garner's role as lieutenant to political boss James Wells. Unfortunately, the treatment of Garner does not extend throughout his career and does not deal with the Garner, Rayburn, Roosevelt relationships.

097. Bailey, Joseph Weldon. Letter to Sam Rayburn, 1 June 1909, Sam Rayburn Library.

Bailey was almost always under attack. He was the equivalent of a lightening rod in politics. In this letter to his protege Sam Rayburn, he attacks his enemies and outlines his hopes to attack them in political debate.

098. Gould, Lewis L. <u>Progressives and Prohibitionists</u>. Austin: University of Texas Press, 1973.

Although this book does not deal with Rayburn, it provides valuable contextual information on the Progressive movement in Texas and on Progressive support for prohibition.

099. Holcomb, Bob Charles. "Senator Joe Bailey, Two Decades of Controversy." Ph.D. diss., Texas Technological College, 1968.

This history dissertation is probably the most thorough and most objective account of Bailey. While Rayburn is not treated in this study, it is invaluable in order to understand Bailey, the formative political influence upon Sam Rayburn.

100. Kornitzer, Bela. <u>American Fathers and Sons</u>. New York: Hermitage House, 1952, pp. 209-221.

This short volume examines the family backgrounds of a number of leading Americans. Based heavily on an interview with Rayburn, it describes Rayburn´s poor, rural upbringing. There is information on his parents and on Rayburn´s attendence at Mayo College. Interestingly, the chapter minimizes the influence of Rayburn´s father upon his life. A useful character sketch is included which, like so many character sketches of Rayburn, emphasizes that he was quiet and shy.

101. Link, Arthur S. <u>Wilson: The New Freedom</u>. Princeton: Princeton University Press, 1956, pp. 425-426.

Rayburn gets little attention in this book on the Wilson Administration; it is too soon in his career for him to be much of a player on the national political scene. However, there is a useful discussion of the Rayburn bill in this volume, its initial adoption by the Wilson Administration, and its ultimate abandonment by the administration.

102. Richardson, Truman. "Sam Rayburn´s First Race for Congress--75 Years Ago," <u>Sam Rayburn Library Newsletter</u> 7 (3): 1-3.

This short article examines Rayburn´s 1912 race for Congress. It points out that Rayburn won that election with only 23.5% of the vote in what was a winner-take-all primary. Rayburn could not have won the election without extremely strong support from Fannin County, his home county. There is also the suggestion that the large number of candidates split other counties´ support from their favorite sons. Friends and neighbors voting, where home counties were relied upon to support candidates, was the predominant voting pattern.

103. Supreme Court of the United States of America, "Admission of Sam Rayburn to the Bar of the Supreme Court," Framed certificate on the wall of the annex building of the Sam Rayburn Library.

When Sam Rayburn was admitted to practice before the U.S. Supreme Court, according to this certificate, he was sponsored by Joseph Weldon Bailey. In order to be admitted to practice before the Supreme Court, the customary procedure is for a lawyer already admitted to the Supreme Court bar to sponsor the aspiring lawyer. Rayburn chose his political mentor as his sponsor.

THE NEW DEAL AND FAIR DEAL

104. Allen, Robert S. Interview with Author, 13 June 1980, Sam Rayburn Library.

Long time political reporter Robert Allen knew Rayburn and O´Connor quite well. Allen had New Deal sympathies and therefore liked Rayburn and disliked O´Connor. His description of O´Connor is both extremely vivid and very negative. Allen wrote several articles favorable to Rayburn and critical of O´Connor during the Majority Leader fight. His wife, Ruth Finney, also a well-known political reporter, was particularly active in writing pro-Rayburn articles during this time. Allen´s oral history is quite useful in providing information on the character of the two men and on the struggle for leadership.

105. Boren, Lyle. Interview with Author, 28 May 1985, Sam Rayburn Library.

Boren, an Oklahoma Congressman, was a family friend of John Nance Garner and a close friend of Rayburn. He helped Rayburn round up support for the Majority Leadership position in 1936 and tried to help Rayburn get the vice presidential nomination in 1944. He discusses those two efforts, along with Rayburn´s relationship with Lyndon Johnson, in this interview.

106. Brown, D. Clayton. "Sam Rayburn and the Development of Public Power in the Southwest," Southwestern Historical Quarterly 70 (2): 140-154.

The article examines Sam Rayburn´s role in the development of the Southwestern Power Administration. It stresses that he was chiefly responsible for the Administration and that he opposed the power companies in order to provide public power. The article also emphasizes Rayburn´s longstanding interest in resource management.

107. Burns, James MacGregor. Roosevelt: The Lion and the Fox. New York: Harcourt, Brace and Company, 1956, p. 341.

This superb treatment of Roosevelt prior to World War II contains little on Rayburn. However, it does provide an excellent context for understanding the New Deal. Additionally, Burns suggests that there was a deal between Roosevelt and Garner such that Garner would accept the vice presidential nomination if Roosevelt would recognize Southern power in Congress and support Sam Rayburn´s effort to become Democratic Leader and later Speaker.

108. Champagne, Anthony. "Sam Rayburn: Achieving Party Leadership," Southwestern Historical Quarterly 90 (4): 373-392.

This article examines the several attempts by Rayburn to become Speaker. It also examines the battle between Rayburn and O´Connor for the Majority Leadership position in 1936. It discusses Rayburn´s failed efforts to gain the Speakership in earlier years and explains his victory in the leadership battle of 1936 by pointing out that Rayburn´s personality, his close relationship with Garner, his reputation as a New Dealer, and strong signals that he was Franklin Roosevelt´s choice for leader were crucial in his successful leadership effort.

109. Cohn, David L. "Mr. Speaker," Atlantic Monthly, 170 (October, 1942): 73-78.

This treatment of the wartime Speaker was so favorable to Sam Rayburn that friends of Rayburn had the article reprinted and distributed at a dinner that was given in Sam Rayburn´s honor. It mostly provides biographical information on Rayburn, discusses his role in the extension of the draft, and concludes that Rayburn "typifies much of what is most attractive in American life" (p. 78). Of note is Cohn´s discussion of Rayburn´s support of the Roosevelt Administration and organized labor at a time when, as Cohn states it, "an anti-labor terrorism swept Oklahoma and Texas" (p. 73).

110. Dickson, Cecil. Telegram to President Franklin D. Roosevelt, 13 August 1939; STE [Early, Stephen T.]. Memo to President [Franklin D. Roosevelt], 15 August 1939; Roosevelt, Franklin D. Memo to Stephen T. Early, undated; Early, Stephen T. Letter to Cecil Dickson, 25 August 1939, President´s Personal File 474 (Sam Rayburn), Franklin D. Roosevelt Library.

This collection of letters and memos is stapled together in a file on Sam Rayburn at the Roosevelt Library. Attached to this exchange is an undated and unidentified newpaper clipping which mentions Rayburn´s support for Garner. What is interesting about this exchange is that Roosevelt had sent previous congratulatory letters to Rayburn on Sam Rayburn appreciation days in the district. In this case, Sam Rayburn Day was to be August 22, 1939; Dickson's request for a message was sent on August 12 and was received by Roosevelt's secretary on August 15. There was plenty of time to send a message; however, Early enclosed the newspaper clipping and asked the President if he wanted to send the message "in light of pro-Garner statements" by Rayburn. Roosevelt responded to Early that he did not want to send a message and suggested language for a letter to Dickson such as, "Sorry--my absence makes it impossible etc." Waiting to respond to Dickson until three days after Sam Rayburn Day, Early wrote that it was impossible to send the message because the President had not received it on time due to a delay in getting the message to him. Claimed Early, "fog and air trouble by Navy pilots" had led to the delay. The exchange is an excellent illustration of the tension created by Garner's break with Roosevelt and the friendship that continued between Rayburn and Garner.

111. Dies, Martin. Interview with A. Ray Stephens, 23 April 1966, North Texas State University.

Dies, a Texas Congressman and well-known demogogue, briefly discussed Rayburn's relationship with Garner. In Dies' view, Garner was a tough master, but Rayburn continued in his apprenticeship and learned and benefited from the relationship.

112. Elsey, George M. Memorandum to Charles Murphy, September 20, 1948, Harry S Truman Papers, Clark M. Clifford files, Harry S Truman Library.

The memorandum notes that Matt Connelly, one of Truman's aides, regarded the whistlestop in Bonham as being the most important speech of the Texas tour. Elsey added that the President was appearing in Bonham at the request of Sam Rayburn and he suggested that Rayburn's advice be sought on appropriate topics for the speech.

113. Farley, James A. <u>Behind the Ballots</u>. New York: Harcourt, Brace and Co., 1938, pp. 133-153.

Farley was a master political operative who had major responsiblity for putting together the Roosevelt coalition. In this useful treatment of political personalities, coalition building, and political organization during the early Roosevelt years, Farley explained how he met with Rayburn and how the Roosevelt-Garner ticket developed from those meetings. Farley noted that Rayburn was a political realist who realized that Roosevelt was the Democratic Convention's candidate and who arranged for the release of the Garner delegates after Roosevelt's strength became clear.

114. Freidel, Frank. <u>Franklin D. Roosevelt: The Triumph</u>. Boston: Little, Brown and Co., 1956, pp. 307-310.

One of the best treatments of Roosevelt and the New Deal, Freidel's book contains a brief, useful treatment of the decision by Garner to release his votes at the 1932 convention. Garner feared a stalemate because he was concerned that it would destroy public confidence and cost the Democrats the election. Additionally, he was satisfied with being Speaker. When Garner released the delegates, he told Rayburn, "Hell, I'll do anything to see the Democrats win one more national election" (p. 309).

115. Gordon, Lester Ira. "John McCormack and the Roosevelt Era." Ph.D. diss., Boston University, 1976, pp. 149-150.

One of the few scholarly works on McCormack, this dissertation is especially valuable in discussing the strong bond that developed between McCormack and John Nance Garner. McCormack, like Garner an avid poker player, was Garner's political arm into New England. Rayburn was allied with McCormack through Garner and also because it was Rayburn who got McCormack admitted to the group of Congressmen who were close associates of Garner. Rayburn aided McCormack in obtaining a seat on the powerful Ways and Means Committee. McCormack, a New England, big city, Irish-Catholic, broke O'Connor's lock on New England's votes in the Democratic Caucus and was probably responsible for Rayburn getting the leadership position.

116. Gosnell, Harold F. <u>Truman's Crises: A Political Biography of Harry S Truman</u>. Westport, Connecticut, 1980, pp. 180-184.

This outstanding volume on Truman notes that Rayburn worked with other Democratic Party leaders to remove Henry Wallace from the Vice Presidential ticket in 1944. While there was an effort to replace Wallace with Rayburn, Rayburn was unable to attain the Vice Presidency and Truman became the replacement.

117. Ickes, Harold L. The Secret Diary of Harold L. Ickes. Vol. 3 The Lowering Clouds 1939-1941. New York: Simon and Schuster, 1955, p. 168.

This volume is the third of a three volume diary of Harold Ickes, an intimate of Franklin Roosevelt. Ickes´ writing tends to be self-serving and, since he was not friendly to Rayburn, one should question his interpretation of Roosevelt´s use of Lyndon Johnson to embarrass Rayburn. Ickes´ brief mention of this incident appears to be the origin of later commentary regarding an effort by Roosevelt forces to displace Rayburn´s influence as a New Deal leader in Texas with young Congressman Lyndon Johnson.

118. McCormack, John. Letter to Sam Rayburn. 20 October 1950, Sam Rayburn Library.

McCormack apparently obtained some unexpected funds to distribute to Congressmen facing reelection because he wrote Rayburn, "I am in a position where I can help a few more members whom you think ought to get it. If you will send me the names at once of three or four I will be able to do so. My purpose in writing you is that I did not want to have any duplication of those we have already helped before we left Washington. I had the names of the eight I wrote to from Boston. You will remember the names of those we helped before we left Washington. I would like to have you send them to me. If you have any others you have particularly in mind, let me know at once."

119. _____. Letter to Sam Rayburn. undated except for the notation "Saturday" with an attached envelope showing a postmark of 28 October 1950, Sam Rayburn Library.

McCormack wrote Rayburn that he had sent $250 to Walter Huber, Harry Davenport, Louis Rabaut, Phil Welch and Sam Yorty. John Dingell got another $250, added McCormack; while Foster Furcolo got another $100.

120. _____. Letter to Sam Rayburn, undated except for the notation "Wednesday," Sam Rayburn Library.

In this letter, McCormack wrote Rayburn that he had given money to twelve Congressmen. They are listed as "Furcolo another $100" and then $250 each to John Dingell, Davenport, Rabaut, Mrs. Woodhouse, Rodino, Addonizio, Howell, Dan Flood, Steve Young, Chester Gorski, and Jim Polk. He added that he had been informed by Harding that $330,000 "has been sent out to members, which does not include what we have sent out."

121. _____. Letter to Sam Rayburn. undated, Sam Rayburn Library.

McCormack wrote Rayburn that he had received $2000 in cash from Floyd Odlum. While Odlum wanted the Democratic National Committee's Finance Committee to know about the contribution, McCormack suggested to Rayburn that they wait until after the election before informing anyone of the contribution. That way, he suggested, they could give the money to their candidates and "it will not interfere with any other possible assistance from the National Committee for some of our candidates." He divided the money into eight sums of $250 each and sent it to Tauriello of New York, Burke of Ohio, Weir of Minnesota, Marshall of Minnesota, Mack of Illinois, Christopher of Missouri, Burnside of West Virginia, and Walsh of Indiana. He asked Rayburn for a letter listing who had been assisted prior to his departure from Washington so that McCormack would not duplicate contributions. He then added, "For your own information I have given Foster Furcolo $500--Harold Donohue $500, and I have helped some Democratic candidates in Massachusetts with $250, and I will help some others. If you know of two to four other boys having a fight, and who need help--whom we have not helped to date--send their names along to me, as I can raise enough to send them $250 from you and I."

122. McDonald, Glenn "T-Bone." Interview with Author, 1 July 1985, Sam Rayburn Library.

McDonald, at the time of the problems over the Denison Dam, was manager of the Chamber of Commerce in Durant, Oklahoma. He was strongly in favor of the dam and worked with Sam Rayburn to reduce Oklahoma's opposition to the dam. This interview provides an insider's account of the problems with Oklahoma over the dam and discusses the role of the utility industry and Governor Phillips in fighting it.

123. Moley, Raymond. <u>27 Masters of Politics in a Personal Perspective</u>. New York: Funk & Wagnalls, 1949, pp. 66-77.

There is a useful chapter on Garner in this volume. It provides a sense of his conservatism, his tenacity, and his stubborness. Moley notes that Garner found Roosevelt unreliable, he disliked Roosevelt´s advisors, and he opposed such Roosevelt policies as the Court-packing plan of 1937 and the Democratic Party purge of 1938.

124. Mooney, Booth. <u>Roosevelt and Rayburn: A Political Partnership</u>. Philadelphia: J.B. Lippincott, 1971.

Mooney, for many years a Johnson staff member, was a close friend of Rayburn. He offers a useful comparison and contrast of Roosevelt and Rayburn and examines Rayburn´s contribution to the New Deal, including his work as chairman of the Interstate and Foreign Commerce Committee. He points out that the alliance between the two men explains much of the legislative success of the New Deal. The weakness of the book is that he tends to overlook tensions in the relationship between the two men, such as tensions involving Rayburn´s loyalty to Garner after Garner´s break with Roosevelt.

125. Parmet, Herbert and Marie B. Hecht. <u>Never Again</u>. New York: Macmillan, 1968.

This book explores the third term for Roosevelt in great detail. Of particular importance to this research is the discussion of the opposition to a third term and the break with John Nance Garner. That opposition forced Roosevelt into a strategy of responding to a draft for a third term. Noteworthy as well, was Roosevelt´s strategy of suggesting many persons as possibilities for the vice-presidency.

126. Patenaude, Lionel V. <u>Texans, Politics and the New Deal</u>. New York: Garland Publishing, 1983.

The strong relationship between Garner and Rayburn is treated in this volume which emphasizes the role of Texas political figures in the New Deal. Of the members of Congress during the New Deal, Rayburn is noted as both being the closest ally of Garner and also being most influential within the New Deal.

127. Patterson, James T. <u>Congressional Conservatism</u> <u>and the New Deal: The Growth of the Conservative</u> <u>Coalition in Congress, 1933-1939</u>. Lexington, Mass.: Lexington Books, 1967, p. 53.

> Valuable in understanding the development of organized opposition to Roosevelt within the Democratic Party, the book stresses the importance of the Public Utility Holding Company Act as being crucial to that emerging opposition. O´Connor and his obstructionist Rules Committee are portrayed as playing a major role in that conservative opposition.

128. Schlesinger, Arthur M. <u>The Politics of Upheaval</u>. Boston: Houghton Mifflin, 1960, p. 383.

> This book provides an excellent discussion of the New Deal. It only briefly mentions opposition to rural electrification, although it does note that the private utility companies were strongly opposed to rural electrification.

129. Shanks, Alexander Graham. "Sam Rayburn and the New Deal, 1933-1936," Ph.D. diss., University of North Carolina at Chapel Hill, 1964.

> This dissertation is a valuable treatment of Sam Rayburn´s role within the New Deal during his chairmanship of the Interstate and Foreign Commerce Committee. In particular, an excellent examination of the politics surrounding railroad holding company, utility holding company, securities, REA, and FCC legislation is offered. From a reading of this dissertation, the central role of Rayburn within the first administration of Franklin Roosevelt becomes clear. The dissertation also contains a useful discussion of Rayburn´s personal life, including an explanation of Rayburn´s divorce which was based on an interview with Rayburn´s associate and biographer, D. B. Hardeman.

130. [Smith, Howard.] Untitled, undated, December, 1936 file, Hatton Sumners Papers, Dallas Historical Society.

> This unsigned document is on Howard Smith´s letterhead. It endorses John O´Connor for Majority Leader in 1936. Although O´Connor was a northern, urban Catholic, Smith apparently preferred O´Connor´s conservatism and unfriendliness to the New Deal to Rayburn´s strong

support of the New Deal. The document is
important in showing a long-standing ideological
division between Smith and Rayburn.

131. Timmons, Bascom N. <u>Jesse H. Jones: The Man and
the Statesman</u>. New York: Henry Holt and Company,
1956, pp. 277-279.

Well known news reporter Bascom Timmons was
friendly with Jones and that may explain this
largely uncritical treatment of the man. The book
does point out that Jones, the candidate of the
last-ditch Garner supporters, split Texas and thus
killed whatever chance Rayburn had for the Vice
Presidency. Interestingly, Timmons notes that
Jones told the Texas delegation that he was going
to withdraw his candidacy because Roosevelt wanted
Wallace on the ticket. Apparently, it was the
first Rayburn had heard that Wallace was the
choice.

132. Truman, Harry. Untitled and undated handwritten
draft of a book review of C. Dwight Dorough´s <u>Mr. Sam</u>
(025), Miscellaneous Historical Documents file, Harry S
Truman Library.

The review shows great affection for Sam Rayburn.
Of particular interest is that part of the review
which states, "As a member of the so-called Big
Four, Sam Rayburn was a tower of strength to the
President of the United States. I can hear him
say time after time when I made a tough statement
on foreign affairs or on legislation pending, ´Now
Mr. President, let´s consider that.´ Well, we
always did and the program was improved by his
views."

133. U.S. Senate. Special Committee to Investigate
Lobbying Activities. <u>Investigation of Lobbying
Activities</u>. 74th Cong., 1st sess., 1935.

These hearings, chaired by Senator Hugo Black of
Alabama, uncovered a massive pattern of lobbying
abuses by the utility industry that ultimately led
to the passage of the Utility Holding Company Act.
Without the investigation by Senator Black, an
investigation which was well-publicized and which
focused attention on the lobbying abuses by the
holding companies, Rayburn would have been unable
to pass more than toothless anti-holding company
legislation in the House.

134. Waller, Robert A. "The Selection of Henry T. Rainey as Speaker of the House," Capitol Studies 11 (2): 37-47.

Relatively little has been written on the politics of leadership selection in the House of Representatives. This article examines how Rainey became Speaker and includes discussion of his alliance with Byrns and the opposition to Rainey by the Garner forces.

THE CONGRESSIONAL DISTRICT

135. Beckham, Vernon. Interview with Author, 17 December 1980, Sam Rayburn Library.

Beckham worked in Rayburn´s behalf in the Denison area and was interested in area politics, eventually becoming a state representative. His interview discusses Rayburn´s campaigns and his campaign style as well as Rayburn´s personality. The interview pointed out Rayburn´s skill in turning political enemies into political friends, one example being M. M. Morrison who had opposed Rayburn, but became a strong Rayburn supporter. Beckham also noted Rayburn´s skill in building an effective political organization over his many years in politics, an organization that sometimes crossed three generations within a family.

136. Champagne, Anthony. Congressman Sam Rayburn. New Brunswick: Rutgers University Press, 1984.

Based heavily on interviews with associates of Sam Rayburn, the book explores the relationship between Rayburn and his Congressional district. It tries to explain how Rayburn survived in office for nearly half a century, especially while leading the national Democratic Party in the House and representing a conservative, rural district.

137. _____. "Sam Rayburn," a speech delivered at the East Texas State University Sam Rayburn Public Affairs Symposium, Commerce, Texas, 29 March 1983.

The speech, on file at the Sam Rayburn Library, provides an overview of Sam Rayburn´s career, particularly as it relates to the Fourth Congressional District. It also describes how Rayburn is remembered and how he projected a folksy image within his Congressional district.

138. Chapman, E. B. Interview with Author, 28 May 1980, Sam Rayburn Library.

Chapman, a leader of the Rayburn forces in Grayson County and son-in-law of Lee Simmons, discussed Simmons´ role in the Rayburn organization. That discussion included Simmons´ work both in promoting the Denison Dam and in protecting Rayburn´s political interests during the land condemnations that were necessary to build the dam and Lake Texoma. He also discussed the Rayburn organization in general, some of Rayburn´s campaigns, and Rayburn´s political style.

139. Cole, Buster. Interview with Author, 21 August 1980, Sam Rayburn Library.

From the late 1940s until Sam Rayburn´s death, Cole was the political leader for Rayburn in Fannin County and coordinated his campaigns throughout the district. It is doubtful that anyone knew Sam Rayburn any better during those years. Cole discussed Rayburn´s personality and his political campaigns. Most importantly, he noted Rayburn´s great reluctance to campaign and reported that he had a genuine dislike of going out and meeting people. However, he eventually would allow himself to be persuaded to do so by Cole. It was Cole who put together such a strong campaign in Rayburn´s behalf in 1948 that he never again was seriously challenged in the Democratic primary.

140. Estes, Kate Reed. Interview with Author, 13 February 1981, Sam Rayburn Library.

Estes, a friend of Rayburn and a political activist, discussed Rayburn´s personality and his concerns with improving the lives of farmers. She especially stressed rural electrification as a major benefit to farmers and offered comparisons of farm life before and after REA.

141. Gee, James. Interview with Judith Kidd Rudoff, 21 March 1980, East Texas State University.

In what appears to be a self-serving interview, Gee claims Rayburn tried to stack the faculty with political friends and that he came into conflict with Rayburn since Gee wanted to increase faculty standards. He claims he confronted Rayburn on the issue and that Rayburn left him alone after that. Gee also noted that the "crowning ignominy" of his work at East Texas was when he fought for years to get a student union building and it was named for Rayburn. For that, he blamed Ray Roberts who was in the state senate and was allied with Rayburn.

142. _____. Letter to Mark Cheeley, 21 November 1963, Box 1.23, Ray Roberts Papers, East Texas State University.

> This letter, with a carbon copy to Ray Roberts, claims that Rayburn's primary activity over the sixteen years that Gee was involved in East Texas State's administration was to try to get Gee fired. Finally, claims Gee, Rayburn gave up, but that was all Rayburn did relating to East Texas State.

143. Hall, Levis. Interview with Author, 29 May 1980, Sam Rayburn Library.

> Hall was a political activist and a close political ally of Rayburn in Sherman, the largest town in the district. Hall offers a carefully reasoned analysis of the political attitudes of the Congressional district, some of Rayburn's political campaigns, and the Rayburn political style. He particularly emphasizes how Rayburn was able to inspire the trust of his constituents.

144. Hardin, Paul. Interview with Author, 5 November 1980, Sam Rayburn Library.

> Hardin was a Rayburn associate within the district. He discussed Rayburn's political style and some of the projects Rayburn brought to the district, including the Denison Dam. Hardin believed that the political repercussions of government land purchases was reduced by other relatively inexpensive land being available in the area.

145. Jordan, Albert. Interview with Author, 5 October 1987, Sam Rayburn Library.

> Jordan was the personnel officer for the Bonham Veterans Hospital and Domiciliary. His interview provides valuable information on the interest taken by Rayburn in all aspects of the staffing of the facility. Most of the positions were under civil service and Rayburn never tried to circumvent the law. However, he stressed with Jordan the importance of filling positions with local people and he made sure that his constituents were aware of position availability and civil service test dates. Interestingly, even the most minor positions interested Rayburn and he made sure that he was kept informed about any

vacancies or any terminations at the hospital and domiciliary.

146. Leslie, Samuel Fenner. Interview with Wayne Little, 26 July 1965, Sam Rayburn Library.

Leslie was a long-time political associate of Rayburn and was one of his closest personal friends. It was Leslie who handled the sensitive matter of Sam Rayburn's divorce and it was Leslie who was one of the men Rayburn trusted to handle the political repercusssions of land purchases for the Denison Dam. Leslie provides a good sense of his relationship with Rayburn and his political functions within the Rayburn organization. He refused, however, to discuss the Rayburn divorce.

147. Martin, Roscoe. <u>The People's Party in Texas</u>. Austin: University of Texas Press, 1970.

Although this slim volume does not focus on Rayburn, it provides an overview of the beliefs of rural populists. It also offers data on the strength of populist voting in Texas. Although Rayburn's district is not at the core of populist strength, there was significant support for populists in his district in the nineteenth century.

148. Nash, Walter C. "Sam Rayburn the Congressman of the Fourth District of Texas." M.A. thesis, East Texas State College, August 1950.

Although poorly written, this thesis captures the farmer image of Sam Rayburn. Nash interviewed Rayburn for his thesis and Rayburn drove him over the countryside in his pickup truck during the interview. Periodically, Rayburn talked about the people of the district and about agriculture. If Nash had not known that he was riding with the Speaker of the House of Representatives, he might have thought he was riding with any Fannin County farmer.

149. Peeler, Ray. Interview with Author, 25 February 1981, Sam Rayburn Library.

Peeler, an attorney in Bonham and a longtime supporter of Sam Rayburn, provides a frank discussion of Rayburn's personality and values along with useful information about the politics of the Fourth Congressional District. He stresses the tradition of populism in the district and

notes that Rayburn had populist leanings.
Additionally, he notes that Rayburn obtained money
from wealthy Texans to give to loyal Democratic
Congressmen who faced campaigns for re-election.

150. Rodes, W. M. (Pete). Interview with Author, 9 May
1980, Sam Rayburn Library.

Rodes was the leader of the Rayburn forces in
Rains County, the least populous county in
Rayburn's district, for many years. The interview
provides excellent information on the Rayburn
political organization and on patronage problems
which Rayburn faced over the years. Even though
Rains County was very small and sparsely
populated, Rodes makes it clear that Rayburn did
not take it for granted in district politics.

151. Saylor, Joe. Letter to Ray Roberts, 7 January
1963, Box 1.23, Ray Roberts Papers, East Texas State
University.

This letter, written to Ray Roberts by a
government professor at East Texas State over two
years after Rayburn's death, expresses the wish
that Gee would retire so that there could be an
appropriate celebration at the dedication of the
Student Union. It is clear from the letter that
there was great tension between Gee and Rayburn.
It praises Roberts for his efforts to insure that
Sam Rayburn's name will be associated with the
Student Union in spite of Gee's efforts

152. Slagle, R. C. Interview with Author, 17 October
1980, Sam Rayburn Library.

Slagle was one of Rayburn's political leaders in
Grayson County and was one of the most influential
politicians in the district. When Rayburn died,
he finished second against Ray Roberts in the
Democratic primary to succeed Rayburn. Slagle's
interview discusses politics in the district,
Rayburn's campaigns, and his thoughts of
retirement if Truman was defeated. Slagle, like
Boyd (012), was approached by people who offered
money if he would oppose Rayburn. Like Boyd,
Slagle refused.

153. Smith, Truett. Interview with Author, 16 May
1980, Sam Rayburn Library.

Smith was one of the leaders of Sam Rayburn's
informal political organization in Collin County.

He provides a good treatment of Sam Rayburn's political style and his values. He concentrates on Rayburn's folksiness and his ability to identify with his poor, small farmer constituency. Indeed, Smith notes that Rayburn seemed to feel that farming was the ideal life.

154. "To the Voters of the Fourth Congressional District." Anonymous campaign leaflet, 1932, Texas and District Political File, Sam Rayburn Library.

This political handbill stresses Rayburn's interest in farming and also his personal honesty. It characterizes an important part of Rayburn's political style which was to emphasize his rural interests and his character.

155. Young, Valton J. The Speaker's Agent. New York: Vantage, 1957.

Written by the county agent for Fannin County, Young was a close friend of Sam Rayburn. The book details Rayburn's intense interest in soil conservation and in agriculture in general.

THE EISENHOWER AND KENNEDY YEARS

156. Aikin, A. M. "Sam Rayburn Memorial Day Speech," 6 January 1978, Sam Rayburn Library.

Aikin was a long time state senator and one of the most respected men in Texas politics. He was also a friend of Rayburn and in this speech, he discusses his role in preventing a redistricting bill from harming Rayburn's interests. Aikin was one of the members of the redistricting subcommittee and, although some of Rayburn's enemies were trying to draw part of conservative Dallas County into Rayburn's district, Aiken prevented it.

157. Banks, Jimmy. Money, Marbles and Chalk. Austin: Texas Publishing, 1971, pp. 113-29.

Banks, a journalist for the Dallas Morning News, provides a largely favorable treatment of Allan Shivers and his role in the pro-Eisenhower movement in both 1952 and in 1956. Much of Banks' essay relies heavily on interviews with Allan Shivers. Little contrasting material is offered.

158. Brademas, John. Interview with Author, 24 June 1980, Sam Rayburn Library.

Brademas discussed the relationship between Rayburn and the liberal wing of the Democratic Party. He noted that while there were tensions, Rayburn was held in great regard by many liberals. Additionally, Rayburn was such an institution in the House of Representatives that liberals could never have seriously considered challenging his power.

159. Carleton, Don E. Red Scare!. Austin: Texas Monthly Press, 1985, pp. 91-92, 137, 267-273.

This examination of anti-communist politics in Texas, and particularly in Houston, in the 1950s shows the importance of Hugh Roy Cullen and his wealth in promoting conservative causes. Cullen became a great supporter of Senator Joe McCarthy and was a large financial contributor to him.

160. Daniel, Price. Interview with Fred Gantt, 25 February 1967, 6 May 1967, and 10 September 1968, North Texas State University.

This lenghty interview with Daniel includes an excellent discussion of the 1956 party battle. According to Daniel, it was Johnson who suggested an alliance to overthrow the influence of the liberal-labor wing of the party. Rayburn was less willing to join with Daniel, apparently doubting Daniel's party loyalty.

161. _____. Interview with Author, 10 January 1980, Sam Rayburn Library.

Daniel served as Speaker of the Texas House of Representatives, Attorney General of Texas, U.S. Senator, Governor of Texas, and, much later in life, as a Texas Supreme Court justice. He was deeply involved in the tidelands dispute. In that dispute, he opposed Rayburn's compromise position on the tidelands and used the issue to advance politically. He also supported Eisenhower for the Presidency in 1952, much to Rayburn's dismay. However, in 1956, he supported Stevenson for the Presidency and joined a coalition with Rayburn and Lyndon Johnson to drive the liberal wing of the Democratic Party from control of the state party. Later, he helped Johnson in his campaign for the Presidency in 1960 and then aided the Kennedy-Johnson ticket in 1960. He discussed all these events in his interview, and he noted that it took some time for Rayburn to trust him in 1956 after his fling with the Eisenhower movement in

Texas. He also noted that Rayburn and he had discussed their service as Speaker of the Texas House of Representatives and that they both held fond memories of the experience.

162. Donovan, Robert J. <u>Eisenhower: The Inside Story</u>. New York: Harper and Brothers, 1956, p. 321.

This useful journalistic treatment of Eisenhower is limited to Ike´s first administration. It notes the struggle Eisenhower and Rayburn were involved in over the $20 income tax cut. Rayburn, Donovan claimed, was irritated when Eisenhower said that the bill reached the "heights of fiscal irresponsibility." Rayburn countered claiming that that it was the Republicans who were irresponsible because they "didn´t give the little folks anything last year and gave the dividend folks theirs." Partisanship of this type, claims Donovan, continued "off and on through the session...."

163. Gossett, Ed. Interview with H.W. Kamp, 27 June and 1 August 1969, North Texas State University Oral History Collection.

Gossett was a conservative Texas Congressman who was never a strong supporter of the Democratic leadership of the House. He was a major Congressional spokesman for Texas´ position in the battle over the tidelands. Gossett provides useful information on the situation in Texas in the tidelands dispute. He also emphasizes his admiration for Rayburn´s character and notes Rayburn´s similarity to Fred Vinson in being unconcerned about personal wealth.

164. Hall, W.G. Interview with Author, 18 December 1980, Sam Rayburn Library.

Hall was a leader of the liberal wing of the Democratic Party and remained friendly with Sam Rayburn and with Lyndon Johnson. In the interview, Hall describes the factions and the politics within the Democratic Party in the 1950s. He told Rayburn that he was certain Shivers was going to support Eisenhower for the Presidency; a thesis that Rayburn rejected. Later, when Shivers did endorse Eisenhower, Rayburn commented upon Hall´s prescience in predicting Shivers´ action.

165. Harris, Oren.   Interview with Author, 3 June 1985, Sam Rayburn Library.

Harris, a representative from Arkansas who became chairman of the Interstate and Foreign Commerce Committee, was closely associated with Rayburn. He discusses his relationship with Rayburn and the politics surrounding the natural gas deregulation bill which was ultimately vetoed by Eisenhower.

166. _____.   Interview with Paige Mulhollan, undated, Lyndon Baines Johnson Library.

A somewhat more extensive interview than the Harris interview at the Rayburn Library (165), it also concentrates on the politics surrounding the natural gas deregulation bill.   Harris also notes that Rayburn and Johnson were very close and that Rayburn promoted Johnson's interests in the Senate and helped him get the Democratic nomination for the Senate in 1948.

167. Ikard, Frank.   Interview with Author, 24 June 1980, Sam Rayburn Library.

Ikard, a Texas Congressman who later became President of the American Petroleum Institute, was very close to Rayburn. He noted that while there were tensions between Texas oil men and Rayburn, Rayburn had many supporters within the oil industry, men who recognized Rayburn's importance to Texas and to the oil industry in spite of Rayburn being perceived as far more liberal than they.

168. Jinks, Harold.   Letter to Dennis Jensen, 17 June 1960, "Party Finances--Texas" file, Box 28, Drexel H. Sprecher Papers, John F. Kennedy Library.

Jinks reported to the Democratic National Committee in this letter that Rayburn promised he would raise $54,000 to pay the remaining Texas debt to the National Committee.   Interestingly, Rayburn apparently promised to raised this huge sum in approximately one month, even though he was also working for Lyndon Johnson's presidential nomination and presumably raising money in Johnson's behalf as well.

169. _____.   Letter to Drexel H. Sprecher, 12 December 1957, "Correspondence--Texas" file, Box 28, Drexel H. Sprecher Papers, John F. Kennedy Library.

This letter suggests that both Lyndon Johnson and Sam Rayburn could tap unlimited funds from oil men, including oil men who had supported Eisenhower. One reason for the return to Democratic loyalties by these oil men, it was claimed, was that the Eisenhower Administration had allowed oil imports to cut into domestic production.

170. _____. Letter to Drexel Sprecher, 2 September 1958, "Correspondence--Texas" file, Box 28, Drexel Sprecher Papers, John F. Kennedy Library.

This letter from a Democratic National Committee official makes it clear just how strongly Rayburn disliked Alger. Numerous Dallas leaders owed Rayburn favors and he was willing to call in those favors to try to get Barefoot Sanders, Alger's 1958 Democratic opponent for Congress, elected. Sanders, however, was unable to defeat Alger in 1958 in spite of Rayburn's efforts in Sanders' behalf.

171. Kimmerling, Harold, M.D. "Medical Report on Sam Rayburn," 2 October 1961, Sam Rayburn Library.

This medical report on Sam Rayburn notes that in 1956, Rayburn suffered a rapid and dramatic loss of vision due to hemorrhaging of the blood vessels in his eyes. From then on, he had very blurred vision and he saw black spots. Vision in his left eye was 8/200 and in his right eye, 20/200. Left eye vision could not be corrected; right eye vision was correctable to 20/40.

172. Kinch, Sam and Stuart Long. Allan Shivers: The Pied Piper of Texas Politics. Austin: Shoal Creek, 1979.

This favorable biography of Shivers by Texas journalists offers a good overview of his life and his role in Texas politics. His involvement in moving Texas into the Eisenhower camp in 1952 and 1956 is thoroughly treated. Oddly, Shivers is portrayed as far more liberal in the policies he pursued than was his conservative image. While the authors' point that Shivers was not a reactionary is a good one, they stress his social welfare spending and ignore his strong states' rights and segregationist orientation.

173. Lucas, Wingate. Letter to Jerry [Gerald] Morgan, 14 October 1957, Wingate Lucas file, Box 1893, Alphabetical Series, Dwight D. Eisenhower Papers, Dwight D. Eisenhower Library.

> In this letter Lucas tells Morgan of a comment Rayburn made about Lucas which was published in Lucas´ "home town paper". Attached to the letter is an unidentified partial article from a newspaper. Rayburn was being interviewed by the newpaper reporter and commented, "I will say the present Democratic delegation from Texas is the finest I ever served with." The reporter responded, "How about Martin Dies?" Rayburn answered, "Oh, he´s just like your Wingate Lucas was. Always votes with the Republicans." "And," asked the reporter, "Fort Worth´s Congressman Wright?" Rayburn stated, "Jim is an able young man who has impressed us all. He´s a comer, has ability and a wonderful personality." The interview is more lengthy, but this part is circled. Lucas wrote Morgan, "These joys I cannot hide: Every other praise beside, I glow, I swell, I burst with pride, For with mine own I now abide." He added in pen at the bottom of the typewritten letter, "Unless you want to send me a copy of your letter to Mr. Rayburn in which you thank him for his compliment of me, don´t reply."

174. _____. Letter to Gerald C. Morgan, 10 March 1958, 41-A Endorsements Bartley, R. file, Box 380, Central--General Collection, Dwight D. Eisenhower Papers, Dwight D. Eisenhower Library.

> In this letter to the General Counsel to the President, Lucas expressed his concern over an article published in the Wall St. Journal which had mentioned that Robert Bartley was going to be reappointed to the FCC. Lucas asked, "[W]hy reward the Speaker, who certainly would not return the favor?" Such an appointment would, Lucas argued, offend "millions of Eisenhower Democrats who hate Rayburn´s guts." It would also add to the belief, claimed Lucas, "that Sam Rayburn has more power now than he had under Truman." Lucas denied that he was a candidate for the FCC, although he did mention interest in the Federal Power Commission, but he noted, "I don´t want my confidence shaken by such cowtowing [sic] to a little man who has always put party above principle."

175. Lyle, John. Interview with Author, 26 February 1980, Sam Rayburn Library.

> Lyle was a close Congressional associate of Rayburn and served on the House Committee on Rules. He knew Garner and knew Rayburn well, especially since his Rules Committee assignment led him to discuss policy matters with Rayburn frequently. This is a particularly valuable interview dealing with Rayburn´s style of Congressional policy making, with concentration on Rayburn´s dealings with a conservative dominated House Committee on Rules during the chairmanship of Adolph Sabath, an ineffective chairman who was a national Democrat. Lyle also discussed Rayburn´s response to Eisenhower´s veto of the natural gas deregulation bill.

176. Moeller, Walter. Interview with Author, 16 May 1984, Sam Rayburn Library.

> Moeller was a junior Democratic Congressman from a very competitive district in the Midwest. Although he did not know Rayburn well, he discovered Rayburn was aware of his Democratic loyalty and also aware of his electoral difficulties in his district. In the midst of his battle for reelection, he opened an envelope from Rayburn and found $1000 in cash from him. That contribution was a very large and needed one for Moeller.

177. Pack, Lindsy Escoe. "The Political Aspects of the Texas Tidelands Controversy." Ph.D. diss., Texas A & M University, 1979.

> One of the most useful and comprehensive treatment of the Texas tidelands controversy, this dissertation offers an excellent picture of the political personalities and interests involved in the dispute. It is clear that the tidelands issue was an emotional one for Texans. This dissertation makes it clear that the issue was a catalyst for driving Texans toward the Republican Party in 1952.

178. Ragsdale, W. B. "Sam Rayburn" file, undated, Sam Rayburn Library.

> Ragsdale was a reporter with U. S. News and World Report. He was a friend of Rayburn and was probably the last reporter to interview Rayburn before his death. He met with Rayburn at his

house in Bonham and, because of Rayburn´s weakened condition, he visited the house on two occasions. Ragsdale recorded what was going on in the house during these visits. Constituents continued to call, Rayburn continued to meet with constituents and to dispense advice, and Rayburn stayed in touch by phone with events in Washington.

179. Shivers, Allan. Interview with Author, 13 August 1984, Sam Rayburn Library.

Shivers explained his reasoning for supporting Eisenhower in this interview. The tidelands issue, although not the only reason for Shivers´ positive feelings toward Eisenhower, was in Shivers´ mind the driving force behind his efforts to turn Texas toward Eisenhower in 1952. He also noted that, in spite of his disagreements with Sam Rayburn, he recognized that Rayburn meant a great deal to Texas and that he would not have been able to actually redistrict Rayburn out of office.

180. _____. Interview with Joe Frantz, 29 May 1970, Lyndon Baines Johnson Library.

In this interview, Shivers discusses his relationship with Lyndon Johnson; part of that relationship involved the party struggles of the 1950s which also heavily involved Rayburn. During the course of the interview, Shivers offers his explanation of the promise that he made to Rayburn. It is an explanation that differs radically from the Rayburn perspective that Shivers lied to him. Of course, it is also possible that Rayburn misunderstood Shivers´ promise and understood it to involve a more lasting commitment, which was not dependent on Shivers meeting with Stevenson after the convention and getting Stevenson to promise to support the Texas position on the tidelands.

181. Skelton, Byron. Interview with T. H. Baker, 15 October 1968, Lyndon Baines Johnson Library.

This lengthy interview provides one of the most thorough treatments of the attitudes and activities of anti-Shivers forces in Texas in 1952 and 1956. Skelton believes that Rayburn initially thought Shivers would support the Democratic nominee and that Rayburn was shocked when Shivers supported Eisenhower. Rayburn claimed he had

Shivers´ word that he would support the Democratic nominee. It is one of the best treatments available on the struggles for control of the Democratic Party in 1952 and in 1956.

182. Sorenson, Theodore C. <u>Kennedy</u>. New York: Harper & Row, 1965, pp. 164, 192-193.

One of the numerous post-assasination books on Kennedy, this one, by one of John Kennedy´s most impressive writers, lacks objectivity about Kennedy. However, it does contain a valuable treatment of the religious issue in the 1960 Presidential race and it offers a plausible interpretation of the effort at the 1960 Democratic convention to create a Kennedy-Johnson ticket. Sorenson feels that Rayburn was anti-Catholic and that he believed a Catholic could not and should not be elected President. However, Sorenson believed that Rayburn changed his mind after he heard Kennedy´s speech about religion and politics which he gave to Protestant ministers in Houston.

183. Weeks, O. Douglas. <u>One Party Government in 1956</u>. Austin: University of Texas, Institute of Public Affairs, 1957.

This short volume is probably the most scholarly and balanced account of the battles over control of the Democratic Party in Texas in 1956. It portrays a tough battle between the Shivercrats on the one hand and labor-liberal-loyalist Democrats on the other. Shivers, however, was in a far weaker position than he was in 1952 because this time he was a lame duck and the labor-liberal-loyalists had planned well.

184. _____. <u>Texas in the 1960 Presidential Election</u>. Austin: The University of Texas, 1961.

Weeks´ short volume offers an excellent analysis of Presidential election politics in Texas in 1960. Kennedy´s religion was important in the race and can explain some of the closeness of the race. The major newspapers also supported the Nixon-Lodge ticket. Additionally, there were concerns that the 1960 Democratic platform was hostile to the oil depletion allowance. However, Weeks noted, "In Texas, however, Johnson did not have undivided support. Many Texas voters no doubt thought of Johnson as having ´sold out´ Texas´ strong conservative interests to

collaborate with Kennedy and the national party.
A Belden Poll published on October 23rd indicated
that only 82 per cent of the Kennedy supporters
were for Johnson, although 28 per cent of the
Nixon supporters were for him. In this same poll
54 per cent were opposed to his dual candidacy"
(p. 53). Elsewhere, Weeks notes that even
reported campaign contributions from Texas in 1960
make a long list and "the donations were generous"
(p. 62); however, there were also unreported
contributions about which no satisfactory data
exist.

185. _____. Texas Presidential Politics in 1952.
Austin: University of Texas, Institute of Public
Affairs, 1953.

Weeks provides what is probably the most scholarly
and objective account of the pro-Eisenhower
movement in Texas in 1952. Shivers, of course,
was in control of state government and of the
Democratic Party machinery and so his role in that
Eisenhower movement was considerable, and was
probably essential to the success of the movement.

186. White, Theodore H. The Making of the President,
1960. New York: Atheneum Press, 1961, pp. 172-177.

This excellent treatment of the 1960 Presidential
election includes some discussion of the selection
of Lyndon Johnson for the vice presidency. White
offers many of the standard political explanations
for the choice--for example, Johnson was a
Southerner, was a Protestant, provided balance to
the ticket, and unified the party. However, he
added that he believed the full story of the
choice of Johnson for the vice presidency remained
to be told.

3

Rayburn as Author

187. "Sam Rayburn Speech," 1912, Sam Rayburn Library.

Apparently responding to a charge that he had profited from his service in the Texas legislature by collecting legal fees from railroads which had legislative business, Rayburn asserted that he had never accepted fees from railroads, although his law partners represented the Santa Fe Railroad. Rayburn claimed his partners had offered to share the Santa Fe fee with him, but he refused in order to avoid a conflict of interest. He also claimed that he never accepted fees from those with legislative business.

188. Congressional Record. 63rd Cong., 1st sess., 1913. Vol. 50, pt. 2, pp. 1247-1249.

Rayburn´s first speech on the floor of the House of Representatives showed a cocky, untraditional side of Rayburn that disappeared in later years. Rayburn clearly aligned himself with Woodrow Wilson in the speech and was quite hostile in his treatment of the Republican Party.

189. Letter to Homefolks, 25 May 1913, Sam Rayburn Library.

In this letter, Rayburn described his trip to Panama. While the Canal was worth seeing, Rayburn was unimpressed with Panama City. He was proud of not getting seasick during the voyage. It was to be one of the few trips he ever made outside of the United States. He preferred being in his

Congressional district when Congress was not in session and he thought foreign travel was politically unwise for Congressmen.

190. "Speech," 19 May 1916, Sam Rayburn Library.

In this speech at an unknown location, Sam Rayburn spoke of growing up on a cotton farm, gathering other crops, and of having "plowed and hoed from sun til sun." He spoke of farmers working cotton for ten to twelve hours a day and then spoke of his aspiration: "I want to make the farm a more attractive place to live...."

191. <u>Congressional Record</u>. 67th Cong., 1st sess., 1921. Vol. 61, pt. 4, pp. 4148-4150.

This speech is but one example of Sam Rayburn as a political partisan. It is a speech on the tariff. He accused the Republican Party of promising the people everything in order to get their votes. He accused the Republicans of being the party of obstruction and attacked the Harding Administration for being a failure. Interestingly, at the time of the speech, Harding had been in the White House for only four and one half months.

192. Letter to Katy [Katherine] Thomas, 2 February 1922, Sam Rayburn Library.

This letter to his sister is only one of a handful of letters of Rayburn which remain from the 1920s. It is also one of the few where Rayburn confesses his dreams and ambitions. After the late twenties, Rayburn either quit writing such confessional letters or none remain.

193. Letter to W. A. Thomas, 19 February 1922, Sam Rayburn Library.

This letter to his brother-in-law, W. A. Thomas, discussed Bailey's failure to recognize that he was finished in elective politics in Texas. It also noted that Thomas' support of Bailey might lead people to connect Bailey and Rayburn too closely. Finally, it suggested that Bailey's continuing forays into politics were hurting Rayburn's political ambitions. The letter is clearly one of a politician who feels that his old political ally now stands in the way of his achieving greater political offices.

194. "Speech in Bonham", 6 June 1922, Sam Rayburn Library.

In this speech, made during one of his toughest campaigns for renomination in the Democratic primary, Rayburn stresses his honesty, lack of wealth, and interest in agriculture. It clearly seems an effort to establish a sense of identification with his constituents.

195. "Speech Opening Campaign of Hon. Sam Rayburn for Re-election to Congress." <u>Bonham Daily Favorite</u>, 6 June 1922, p. 4.

In this speech, Rayburn stressed his Southern values, his Confederate heritage, and his support for segregation. He accused his opponents of trying to use blacks to gain votes in the primary, but noted that blacks would not be voting in the primary.

196. "Speech at Windom School," May 1928, Sam Rayburn Library.

Rayburn seems like a demogogue in this speech which was given in a small town in his district. For those more familiar with the taciturn Rayburn of later years, the speech suggests quite a contrast with the younger Rayburn. Speaking to a full house, Rayburn claimed he was a country boy who had learned a few things about the national government in the past sixteen years. He noted that the Wilson Administration had been an honest one, but that the Harding Administration was filled with dishonest men, most of whom had been retained by President Coolidge. He stated that Herbert Hoover either had knowledge of the Teapot Dome scandal and did nothing about it, or that he was not mentally capable of being President. He added that no person had every accused Herbert Hoover of being a fool and then asked his audience to draw their own conclusions. Rayburn then went into great detail about the Teapot Dome scandal. Rayburn argued that the corruption of the Republicans was proof that people were better off staying with the Democratic Party which believed in the masses. He added that he would stand with the principles of his father who was a Confederate veteran and stay with the party of the South. Herbert Hoover, he stressed, had made a deal with Northern Negroes. He had issued an order as Secretary of Commerce to compel equality between Negroes and whites. In exchange for this order, claimed Rayburn, Hoover got the Negro vote for his nomination at the Republican convention. Rayburn claimed that Hoover´s story was untrue that Coolidge had forced him to integrate the rest rooms of the Dept. of Commerce.

197. Letter to Will H. Evans, 16 April 1932, Sam Rayburn Library.

Rayburn urged Evans, a Grayson County political activist, to send a solidly pro-Garner delegation to the Democratic State Convention. At the state convention, he felt an appropriate platform could be written and that Garner would control the state. Rayburn urged Evans to avoid controversial issues like prohibition in the fear that it would hurt Garner´s chances. Rayburn then discussed the prospects for Garner getting the Presidential nomination. He wrote, "He [Garner] has a good chance to get the nomination if Mr. Roosevelt, who appears to be the leading candidate, is stopped, which a great many people say he is. I hardly know where the Convention would go except to Garner if they fail to nominate Rooveselt [sic]." Rayburn seemed to realize, however, that Garner´s chances for the Presidential nomination were slim because he added, "It is at least a great thing for Texas to have one of its citizens even proposed for the nomination to this high office."

198. Letter to William Bankhead, 25 July 1932, Sam Rayburn Library.

This letter is a good indication of the friendship between Bankhead and Rayburn. After Bankhead notified Rayburn that he would likely be a candidate for the Speakership at the beginning of the 1933 session, Rayburn responded that John McDuffie of Alabama might also be a candidate and that Texas newspapers were saying that Rayburn was a "possible, if not a probable" candidate for the Speakership as well. Rayburn confessed that if he were not a candidate, he would feel in a dilemma since he was close to both McDuffie and to Bankhead. He also stressed that he did not want any conflict with either McDuffie or with Bankhead. As he wrote, "I cannot conceive, however, of my coming in conflict with any ambition of yours or McDuffie´s and believe that we can easily straighten out any conflict that might come up."

199. Congressional Record. 74th Cong., 1st sess, 1935. Vol. 79, pt. 9, pp. 10315-10326.

In this House debate over the Public Utility
Holding Company bill, Rayburn presented the
problems that the bill sought to address and then
explained how the bill would resolve those
problems. He also stressed how controversial the
bill had been. In introducing the legislation, he
pointed out that the bill had "been more
misrepresented through propaganda in the mail, by
telegrams, and advertisements in the newspapers
than any bill that has had the consideration of
this Congress in the last half century." He
asserted that people´s motives had been
criticized, and that there had been much gossip,
and numerous advertising campaigns related to the
bill. He added, "In my own state I know that
circulars were put out through the mails and
placed in envelopes with electric-light bills in
which every paragraph of the advertisement or the
circular either contained an unknowing or
deliberate misrepresentation of the facts with
reference to this bill." Later in introducing the
bill, he added, "I want to say to the Committee
now that so far as I am concerned, after all of
the pummeling and the pounding of the last 5
months, I have not changed my position on the
essential aspects of the bill as originally
introduced" (p. 10316). Later in his discussion
of the bill, Rayburn noted that a propaganda
campaign had been developed in Texas in which it
was claimed Rayburn had nothing to do with writing
the bill, that he had not seen it until it was
handed to him. Additionally, the propaganda
claimed that Rayburn really didn´t care whether or
not the bill passed. Rayburn insisted that he did
want the bill to pass and that he and his
committee, particularly through the investigations
of Dr. W. W. Splawn who was a staff member of the
Committee on Interstate and Foreign Commerce and a
crucial advisor to Rayburn during this time, had
played a major role in developing the bill. He
added that the propaganda was "not only false, it
is infamous" (p. 10325). Rayburn must have felt
some bitterness over this propaganda campaign
because he singled out John W. Carpenter, the
president of Texas Power & Light Company, by name
and called him and the presidents of other
subsidiary utility companies "little more ... than
glorified office boys..." (p. 10326).

200. Letter to William Gibbs McAdoo, 23 February 1938,
Sam Rayburn Library.

McAdoo wrote a lengthy letter to Rayburn which
outlined his recollections of the 1932 Democratic
Convention and the arrangement to nominate a
Roosevelt-Garner ticket. He asked Rayburn if he
agreed with those recollections. Rayburn
responded with his own recollections of the
Convention. Rayburn recalled that he and McAdoo,
who led the Garner forces within the California
delegation, had many conversations during the 1932
Democratic Convention. Those conversations
included discussions of the possibility of and the
timing of a release of the Texas and California
delegations to vote for Roosevelt. Late in the
afternoon of the day that Roosevelt was nominated,
claimed Rayburn, McAdoo called a caucus of the
California delegation and Rayburn caucused the
Texas delegation. While the Texas delegation met,
Rayburn left the Texas caucus to find a telephone
to call Garner. As he was in the hall, he met
McAdoo who told him, "What are we going to do? We
will vote for Jack [Garner] until hell freezes
over if you or he says so." Rayburn, prior to
speaking to Garner, told McAdoo, "Go on in and
release your delegation as I am going to the
telephone right now to ask Mr. Garner to give me
the authority to release the Texas Delegation."
Garner did give Rayburn the authority to release
the Texas delegation, but Rayburn noted that the
Texas caucus seemed as if it lasted a long time.
The California delegation acted more promptly and
made it back to the convention floor prior to the
Texas delegation. Rayburn added, "I had known
since the middle of the afternoon of that day that
Mr. Garner was willing and really wanted the
California-Texas Delegations to be released and
had expressed the hope that they would vote for
Mr. Roosevelt, but there were some other things
that had to be done before the release was made."

201. "Speech Seconding the Nomination of Henry Wallace
for the Vice Presidency of the United States." In
Proceedings of the Democratic National Convention,
1940, p. 226.

This brief seconding speech uses language
suggesting a genuine lack of enthusiasm for
Wallace. Rayburn states that he made the
seconding speech out of loyalty to Franklin
Roosevelt and out of respect for Roosevelt's
wishes. He probably is referring to Garner when
he mentions that his heart would have him nominate
another.

202. "Fannin County Speech," 1947, Sam Rayburn Library.

This variation upon the well known "Four cent cotton" speech of Sam Rayburn is a good indication of how Rayburn appealed to his constituents. There is much emphasis upon the improvements in the lives of farmers that resulted from the Democratic Party and there is stress that continued prosperity requires continued Democratic loyalties.

203. "Speech," 31 May 1948, Sam Rayburn Library.

In this statement, Rayburn declared his opposition to "the whole civil-rights program." He added that he had voted against all laws that had appeared to attack segregation. No vote had been held on the civil rights bill in 1948, claimed Rayburn, because there was concern that Republicans and Northern Democrats would join together to pass the bill. However, he had proven his opposition to civil rights by his earlier votes against anti-lynching legislation in the 67th, 75th, and 76th Congresses. He concluded, "If the opposition desires to go on saying that I am for the civil-rights program in the face of this record then the people will know that they are deliberately distorting and falsifying my record."

204. Letter to Curlee Cummings, 23 February 1949, Sam Rayburn Library.

The letter is unusually revealing of the tension between President Gee and Sam Rayburn. Rayburn wrote that in the fall of 1948, he had been approached by some people in Commerce, Texas, the town in which the college is located, to help with establishing an R.O.T.C. unit at the college. Those people appeared concerned that Rayburn would not be of assistance since President Gee had opposed him in the 1948 Democratic primary. Rayburn told them that he still retained his loyalty to the college and that he would help in any way that he could; however, he did not want to deal with President Gee. Another individual, Frank Young, was assigned to work with Rayburn and an R.O.T.C. unit was established. To Rayburn's amazement, he received a long thank you letter from President Gee which suggested the differences between the two men were minimal. Yet, at almost the same time, he learned that President Gee had spoken in Dallas "about the destruction of the

government and abandoning our historic good way of
life." As Rayburn closed the letter, he noted
that he had not decided whether he wanted to
respond to Gee and that just as Gee had no sense
of indebtedness toward Rayburn, Rayburn felt no
indebtedness toward Gee.

205. Letter to Ben F. Tasto, 25 September 1950, Sam
Rayburn Library.

In a letter responding to Tasto´s assessment of
the speaking skills of politicians, Rayburn
offered a positive assessment of Franklin
Roosevelt as a speaker, describing him as "one of
the most compelling speakers I ever heard before
an audience." However, his greatest praise was
for the late Joe Bailey who he regarded as the
most charismatic personality and the best public
speaker he had ever known. Given the vast range
of Rayburn´s political contacts by 1950, it was
extraordinary praise.

206. Letter to John McCormack, 20 October 1950, Sam
Rayburn Library.

Rayburn wrote McCormack that he had received $2500
from a mutual friend and that he had given $250
each to "Sheppard of California, Murdock of
Arizona, Ramsey of West Virginia, Marsalis of
Colorado, Wilson of Oklahoma, Granger of Utah,
Bailey of West Virginia, Walter of Pennsylvania,
Aspinall of Colorado." He stated that he would
give George Wilson another $250 when he went to
Oklahoma on October 21. Apparently, he could not
recall who received the last $250 since he wrote
McCormack, "It´s possible I´ve given $250 to
someone else whose name I can´t remember at the
moment. If I think of who it was, I´ll let you
know."

207. Telegram to John McCormack, 20 November 1952, Sam
Rayburn Library.

In this telegram, Rayburn explained to McCormack
that he changed his mind and that he would serve
as the minority leader of the House of
Representatives. The relevant part of the
telegram states, "Since my conversation with you
on the telephone several days ago at which time
you urged me to accept the Democratic leadership
of the 83rd Congress, I have received many
telegrams, letters and telephone calls from
Democratic members urging me to accept the

leadership if offered. The Democratic members of the Congress have in the past been so fine and generous with me I cannot feel myself justified in denying their request at this time so I have decided that if the position is offered me in the Democratic Caucus I will accept."

208. Letter to Dwight D. Eisenhower, 6 June 1953, Sam Rayburn file, Box 952, President's Personal File, Dwight D. Eisenhower Papers, Dwight D. Eisenhower Library.

Thanking the President for a courtesy note inquiring about his sister's health, he noted that she would be well soon and that she was the mother of Robert Bartley. He added that she was grateful for her son's reappointment and that "you could not have done anything in the world for me that I would appreciate more than the reappointment of Bartley. I shall always remember this as a gracious and fine act on your part."

209. Letter to Willie J. Denson, 14 June 1954, Sam Rayburn Library.

Rayburn noted the first <u>Brown v. Board of Education</u> decision and, while he stressed that he continued to support segregation, "the Supreme Court has spoken, and it is the last word." He concluded by expressing the hope that the Court will allow time for desegregation to become accepted.

210. Letter to George Mahon, 6 December 1954, Sam Rayburn Library.

In this letter to West Texas Democratic Congressman Mahon, Rayburn confessed his dismay over Bruce Alger's behavior. He noted that Alger visited with him and then wrote Rayburn "a very generous letter, and said he wanted to cooperate with the Texas Delegation as far as he could, being a Republican." Rayburn said that after he read Alger's letter, he saw a newpaper clipping which said that Alger had said that Rayburn "placed the welfare of the party before the welfare of the country...." Rayburn added that he thought that showed a lack of wisdom on Alger's part.

211. Interview with V.J. Young, 1956, Sam Rayburn Library.

This interview with county agent V.J. Young was apparently done in preparation for Young's book, The Speaker's Agent (155). Rayburn discussed his rural upbringing with Young. Farm life near the turn of the century was a hard life and Rayburn knew those hardships, remembered them, and resolved to improve the lives of farmers. Most importantly, the strong influence of Joe Bailey upon his political career is recalled by Rayburn.

212. "A Teacher Who Seized Time by the Forelock." National Education Association Journal 49 (3):25.

When one considers how rare it was for Rayburn to write, this brief tribute to President Mayo of Mayo College is particularly noteworthy. Rayburn gives Mayo credit for providing him and others like him with otherwise unobtainable educational opportunities. He also stressed that Mayo inspired him and persuaded him that to succeed in life he must both work hard and have goals.

213. Letter to Elder Floy Gross, 4 August 1960, Sam Rayburn Library.

In response to Elder Gross' concern that Kennedy could not "own [sic] allegiance to the Pope of Rome and at the same time be a fully loyal American citizen," Rayburn wrote that he disagreed. In his folksy style, Rayburn explained that the country was founded on freedom of religion and that no man's religion should be held against him in any race for office. He stressed that Kennedy had performed heroically in World War II and that a man who would willingly offer his life for his country could not be expected to be untrue to it. Rayburn then argued, "[B]eing a Baptist of the hard shell type, ... I have no religious prejudices. I have served in Congress with hundreds of Catholics. By no speech they ever made, nor vote they ever cast, did they indicate they were Catholic, Protestant or Jew. I know this statement is true." He then pleaded with Elder Gross to reconsider and to vote for the candidate who, regardless of religion, would best serve the country.

214. Letter to Foster Phipps, 13 September 1960, Sam Rayburn Library.

The letter explains that although he passed his bar examination, Rayburn practiced little law largely because he ran for reelection to the state legislature in the same year that he passed the bar.   In 1910, he ran again for reelection and then in 1911 was busy being Speaker.   In 1912, he ran for Congress and then had to run every two years thereafter.   According to Rayburn, politics, his first ambition, occupied so much of his time that there was never time to practice much law. Late in his life, he wrote his will and he relied on a Bonham law firm rather than himself to write it (see, Ray Peeler interview, 149).

215. Letter to Darrell Jones, 27 September 1960, Sam Rayburn Library.

In response to another letter expressing concern over Kennedy´s Catholicism, Rayburn wrote, "I cannot agree with you that Kennedy should ever say, under any circumstances, that he would give up his church, any more than I think a Baptist should say it."   He noted that if a Protestant said he would abandon his church in performance of a political duty, he would be condemned.   Given that, he argued, we should not expect Kennedy to say that he would abandon the Catholic faith.

216. "Last Will and Testament," 16 December 1960, Sam Rayburn Library.

The bulk of Rayburn´s estate was land, much of which was purchased by mortgage when land values were depressed.   The entire estate was valued at $300,000.   Books, papers, mementos and the family home were left to the Sam Rayburn Library. Siblings, nieces and nephews received the remainder of the estate.

217. Interview with Dwight Dorough, 27-28 December 1960, Sam Rayburn Library.

In a broad ranging interview, Rayburn discussed his opinions of historical figures and political figures that he had known.   At one point during the interview, Dorough commented that the race question seemed to be the primary problem in the South.   Rayburn, who throughout the interview had been obviously careful in his statements, even to the point of being uncritical of Warren G. Harding, briefly revealed some of his deep seated values.   He compared racial prejudice to the religious prejudice he had just seen in the 1960 Presidential campaign.   Then he said, "I just...I...I just feel terrible when people preach hates for any class or any group or any sect.   I

want everyone to choose their own way to get to
heaven as far as I am concerned.... The only
thing I never mentioned this race question in
public. I feel this way. I feel that the average
person around Bonham thinks its coming, feels sure
it is, because it´s the law. But they want to
give them time enough to get used to...to kind of
get used to it. And, I think the Supreme Court
meant that when it said with deliberate speed and
that may be slow. But, there were a group of
people, colored and more whites, who wanted to
grab the bits in the teeth and run the whole
distance the first dash." After another question,
Rayburn added, "But it is a thing, a progressive
thing, you´ve got to get people used to it. I
thank God that I am one human being that has no
racial or religious prejudices in my life. A man
can´t help being a Negro. Any more than I can
help being born. And, they are certainly human
beings." Although he felt that it was unwise for
radicals to push for speeding up the process of
desegregation, he also saw the danger to racial
tolerance from the strong segregationists, briefly
commenting that the elections in Mississippi the
previous month had been "terrible." In that
election, strong segregationists dominated the
election. It was, without a doubt, a far
different perspective on the race question than
Rayburn had in the 1920s or even the 1940s. Even
on race and religion, probably the two most
emotional issues for Southerners of Rayburn´s
generation, Rayburn was open to change and was
receptive to new ideas.

218. "The Speaker Speaks of Presidents." <u>New York
Times Magazine</u>, 4 June 1961.

In an article written near the end of his life,
Rayburn recalled the Presidents he had known
during his half century in American politics.
There is nothing particularly revealing about
Rayburn or about the Presidents he knew. What is
striking from the discussion, however, is the
sense one gets of the vast time span during which
Rayburn was on the political scene.

4

Archival Sources

Because Sam Rayburn held office for so many years, was involved in many major political controversies, and was the leader of the Democratic Party in the House from 1940-1961, almost any collection of papers of leading national or Texas political figures will have some mention of Sam Rayburn or correspondence with Rayburn. Unfortunately, much of that correspondence is unrevealing. Often, the correspondence involves little more than an exchange of social pleasantries such as birthday greetings. Much correspondence involves notes about fishing trips and fish caught--Rayburn was an avid fisherman. Sadly, little written material reveals much about Rayburn's innermost thoughts or his political strategies. His life and thoughts were surprisingly private when compared with the flood of information available on such contemporaries as Lyndon Johnson and Richard Nixon.

Rayburn did much of his business in person or over the phone. He did not keep memoranda of his conversations or of his promises. Apparently, he relied solely upon his unusually retentive memory. As Lyndon Johnson described Rayburn's style of doing business, "He runs his office out of his back-ass pocket." The result, of course, is that much material which would have been useful to understanding Sam Rayburn died with him.

Other material that is in written form is often indecipherable because of the highly personal, memory-based way in which Rayburn worked. Frequently, in going through material in the files of the Sam Rayburn Library, I found envelopes with several words or a sentence written on them in Rayburn's scrawl;

however, it was impossible to know the matter that
Rayburn had noted. I also found lists of names,
sometimes with lines through the names, sometimes with
plusses or minuses next to the names. Yet, one could
not determine from those records why the lists existed
or why the names had been marked.

No telephone logs were kept by Rayburn or his staff.
Appointment books, even if they existed, would be
useless since Rayburn frequently saw people without
appointments and would speak with people outside the
office, for example, while he was taking his regular
walks in the Capitol area, in the Board of Education
where everything was off the record, and at dinner
after the Board of Education meetings ended. His style
of office management to this observer was remarkably ad
hoc and disorganized; yet, it worked well for Rayburn.
For the scholar interested in studying Rayburn,
however, it creates many frustrations. The result is
that the useful record of Rayburn's thoughts and
interactions is a limited one.

Even Rayburn's speeches provide only a limited record
of his thoughts. For one, his speeches outside the
district were few, even during the last decades of his
life. Unlike many other Southern politicians, oratory
was not his strong point and he was a consensus-maker
and a deal-maker rather than a speech-maker. In 1973,
James R. Haney wrote an M.A. thesis at Abilene
Christian College. In that thesis, he tried to study
Rayburn's speeches in order to gain an understanding of
Rayburn. He was frustrated by the lack of a written
record of Rayburn's speeches. Haney wrote, "Many of
his speeches, perhaps most of them, were made without
manuscripts or notes and would not appear in the speech
files. Especially is this true in regard to his less
formal speaking to agricultural groups, often scarcely
more than personal conversation. Many of these were
not noted in the news media after they were made" (p.
60). Haney added that even "Rayburn's public addresses
consisted of informal talks more than prepared
addresses" (p. 61). Since he was seldom on the floor
of Congress and since his speeches in general were few,
brief, simple, and often abrupt, as Haney discovered
(pp. 113-117), it is difficult to understand Sam
Rayburn through his public statements.

In my own view, one of the most useful tools with which
to understand Sam Rayburn is through the oral histories
which have been provided by persons closely associated
with Rayburn. The most numerous and most valuable oral
histories involving Rayburn are filed in the Sam
Rayburn Library and in the Lyndon B. Johnson Library,

although some useful oral histories may be found in such libraries as the North Texas State University Library, the Harry S Truman Library, and the Dwight D. Eisenhower Library.

With these cautionary notes in mind, the following identifies some of the archival sources where useful information can be found. It also identifies possible sources of new information about Rayburn and mentions some sources where one would expect useful information only to find little or none.

1.   Alabama Department of Archives and History, Montgomery, Ala. The William Brockman Bankhead Papers.

There is some useful correspondence between Rayburn and Bankhead in these files. Most of the correspondence deals with their leadership ambitions. Both men were ambitious to lead the Democratic Party in the House, but they were friends and they maintained a friendly correspondence over several Speakership elections. Once Bankhead was Speaker and Rayburn was his Floor Leader, the correspondence centers on election outcomes and anticipated problems. There are also newspaper clippings with some useful information on several Speakership and Floor Leadership races. Some of these materials mention Rayburn.

2.   Carl Albert and Western History Collection, University of Oklahoma, Norman, Ok. Papers of Speaker Carl Albert and several other Congressmen, primarily from Oklahoma.

As the Albert papers are indexed, they are likely to prove valuable to the Rayburn scholar since Albert was one of Rayburn closest proteges in the House of Representatives. The papers of Lyle Boren and Wilburn Cartwright are among the most useful to Rayburn scholars. They provide a great deal of material on the Denison Dam and the controversy in Oklahoma which surround the construction of the dam and of Lake Texoma. Rayburn is frequently mentioned in any materials involving the dam's construction since he was the primary political force behind its construction.

3.   University of Arkansas Library, Fayetteville, Ark. Papers of Oren Harris, J.W. Fulbright, and Joe Robinson.

Although the Joe Robinson papers contain nothing of value between Robinson and Rayburn, they are invaluable in understanding the effect upon Southern politics of

Al Smith´s candidacy in 1928. J.W. Fulbright´s papers
contain some correspondence with Rayburn and some about
Rayburn in reference to the Southwestern Power
Administration, a public power program in which Rayburn
had great interest and which was opposed by private
utilities. Oren Harris was personally close to Rayburn
and was the House sponsor of controversial natural gas
deregulation legislation which Rayburn supported.
However, the papers provide very little of value to the
Rayburn scholar.

4.   Dallas Historical Society, Dallas, Tx. The Joseph
       Weldon Bailey Papers, the Hatton Sumners Papers,
       and the Tom Love Papers.

The Bailey papers are extensive, although there is only
a smattering of materials which involve correspondence
with Sam Rayburn. Primarily the papers are useful for
understanding Bailey´s political strength, his
political speeches, character, and finances. These
materials help provide a context for Rayburn´s
tremendous admiration for Bailey. Hatten Sumners
represented Dallas County during many of the years that
Rayburn was in Congress. For the most part, the
Sumners papers are unrevealing and there is only
limited correspondence between Rayburn and Sumners.
There is a useful set of newspaper clippings on Sumners
in which Rayburn is frequently mentioned. The Tom Love
Papers provide only a small amount of material dealing
with Rayburn, although they are useful in understanding
Texas politics in the early years of the twentieth
century.

5.   East Texas State University Library, Commerce, Tx.
       James Gee Papers, Ray Roberts Papers and A.M. Akin
       Papers.

One can obtain a sense of the conservatism of James
Gee, President of East Texas State College and
political enemy of Sam Rayburn, from his papers. There
is, however, very minimal correspondence between
Rayburn and Gee. A very useful oral history with Gee
provides insight into the tension between the two men.
Ray Roberts worked for Rayburn and later succeeded him
in the House of Representatives. His papers are
useful to illustrate the intensity of the feelings of
Gee against Rayburn. Roberts, who had a good personal
relationship with Gee, received many letters from
Rayburn´s friends protesting Gee´s unwillingness to
call the student union by its official name, the Sam
Rayburn Student Union. Roberts worked to convince Gee
to be less vengeful. A.M. Akin, a long-time, highly
respected state senator, was a friend of Rayburn who

worked to prevent Rayburn from being redistricted and given part of conservative, Republican Dallas County. There is a small amount of correspondence between Rayburn and Akin.

6.   Dwight D. Eisenhower Library, Abilene, Kn. Presidential Library containing material relevant to the life of President Eisenhower and his administration.

Surprisingly little correspondence is found between Rayburn and members of the Eisenhower Administration. There are logs which show frequent business and social meetings between Eisenhower and Rayburn. Most of these meetings are not recorded, however. Where summaries are made of the meetings, Rayburn is rarely noted as speaking. There are a small number of oral histories which are useful to the Rayburn scholar, especially interviews with General Lucius Clay, who was the officer in charge of the Denison Dam, and interviews with persons who had ties to politics in Texas, such as Joe Ingraham and Jack Porter.

7.   Lyndon B. Johnson Library, Austin, Tx. Presidential Library containing material relevant to the life and administration of President Lyndon Johnson.

The most extensive material on Rayburn found outside of the Sam Rayburn Library is found in the Johnson Library. There is a great deal of correspondence between Johnson and Rayburn, much of it indicating the strong mentor-protege relationship between the two men. There are also frequent mentions of Rayburn in correspondence between Johnson and other Texas political figures. Of special value are oral histories with Texas political figures during the 1940s and especially the 1950s. Rayburn is frequently mentioned in these interviews and they are useful in providing a context for the Johnson-Rayburn political partnership during the Eisenhower years. There is some material on the 1960 Presidential election, but it is less valuable and less revealing than the Kennedy Library's material.

8.   John F. Kennedy Library, Boston, Ma. Presidential Library containing material relevant to the life and administration of President John Kennedy.

There are extremely useful materials in this library dealing with conditions in Texas during the 1960 Presidential campaign. Material discussing the Johnson campaign for the Presidency almost invariably mention Rayburn's importance in the Johnson Presidential

effort. Rayburn's ability to garner campaign funds
from wealthy Texans is also mentioned. Of particular
note is a substantial amount of material on the
religious issue in 1960, including the importance of
Kennedy's Catholicism to Texans. One of the most
valuable collections for the Rayburn scholar in the
Kennedy Library are the Drexel Sprecher Papers.
Sprecher was with the Democratic National Committee and
his papers contain a great deal of information on Texas
politics in the 1950s and 1960 and on Rayburn's role as
a Texas political leader and fund-raiser. The oral
histories at the Kennedy Library supply little on
Rayburn that is of value.

9.   North Texas State University, Denton, Tx. Oral
      history collection.

The Library has a small collection of oral histories,
some of which are very relevant to the study of Sam
Rayburn. Of particular value are oral histories with
Allan Shivers, Price Daniel, Martin Dies, Ed Gossett,
and Alla Clary, all of whom played important roles in
Rayburn's career.

10.   W.R. Poage Congressional Library, Waco, Tx.
      Congressional Library containing the papers of
      several members of Congress associated with Sam
      Rayburn.

The library is relatively new and is still in the
process of obtaining papers and indexing them. There
appear to be only scattered correspondence involving
Rayburn in these collections. There is a very lengthy,
wide ranging oral history with Congressman Poage which
mentions Rayburn and which provides useful contextual
information.

11.   Franklin D. Roosevelt Library, Hyde Park, NY.
      Presidential Library containing material relevant
      to the life and administration of President
      Franklin D. Roosevelt.

There is correspondence between members of the
Roosevelt Administration and Rayburn, although that
correspondence is not extensive. There are also
numerous records of meetings between Roosevelt and
Rayburn, although these meetings are almost invariably
off-the-record. The file on Lyndon Johnson shows the
development of a strong relationship between Roosevelt
and Johnson. There is also some evidence of tension
between Roosevelt and Rayburn when Garner broke with
the administration and ran for President in 1940. The
Library's oral history collections are extensive, but
their relevance to Sam Rayburn is exceedingly limited.

12. Sam Rayburn Library, Bonham, Tx. Papers of Sam Rayburn.

This privately endowed library contains the papers of Sam Rayburn. Relatively few papers exist prior to 1940 as a result of the disappearance of some of Rayburn's files while he was exchanging offices with his Republican counterpart, Joe Martin. The bulk of Rayburn's papers relate to constituent matters, although there are some letters dealing with national policy questions and some letters, particularly a handful of letters to family members during Rayburn's youth, that are very revealing of his feelings and ambitions. There is a substantial quantity of bound newspaper clippings files on Rayburn which range from local papers to major Washington and New York newspapers. The library also possesses approximately 80 oral histories with friends and associates of Sam Rayburn. Each of those interviews concentrates on the interactions between Rayburn and the interviewee. Although the interviews concentrate on Rayburn in his district as opposed to Washington, many of the interviews reveal much of Rayburn's personality. Work at this library is essential for any scholar seriously studying the life of Sam Rayburn.

Donald C. Bacon, co-author with the late D.B. Hardeman of Rayburn: A Biography (see, 039 in the Bibliography), currently possesses approximately thirty linear feet of material on Rayburn. Much of this material was gathered by D.B. Hardeman during the years that Hardeman worked for Rayburn and the many years that Hardeman worked on a biography of Rayburn. According to the provisions in D. B. Hardeman's will, these materials are to be donated to the Sam Rayburn Library. This material has not been viewed by scholars other than Bacon and Hardeman. It promises to be the most valuable source of new material on Rayburn, especially since it includes lengthy interviews between Hardeman and Rayburn. It also contains interviews with key, now deceased, New Deal figures such as Tom Corcoran and Benjamin Cohen. The quality of Rayburn: A Biography, suggests that this new material will be a scholarly gold mine for Rayburn scholars and for Congressional scholars in general.

13. Harry S Truman Library, Independence, Mo. Presidential Library containing material relevant to the life and administration of President Harry S Truman.

The Truman Library contains some very useful materials on Sam Rayburn. There is some material written by

Truman that shows a close, friendly relationship between he and Rayburn. The planning materials for Truman´s whistlestop tour of Texas also show a strong dependence upon Rayburn for advice, support and friendship. Some of the oral histories provide valuable information on Rayburn--probably the most useful being oral histories by Rayburn´s longtime friends Tom Clark and Marvin Jones.

Index

About the Author

ANTHONY CHAMPAGNE received his Ph.D. degree from the University of Illinois in 1973. Currently, he is Professor in the School of Social Sciences at The University of Texas at Dallas. He has published several articles on Sam Rayburn, done over eighty oral histories on Sam Rayburn for the Sam Rayburn Library, and is the author of *Congressman Sam Rayburn* (1984).